Mastering Softball

Ed Zolna and Mike Conklin

Contemporary Books, Inc.
Chicago

Library of Congress Cataloging in Publication Data

Zolna, Ed.
    Mastering softball.

    Includes index.
    1. Softball.   I. Conklin, Mike, joint author.
II. Title.
GV881.Z64   1981   796.357′8   80-70639
ISBN 0-8092-7184-2
ISBN 0-8092-7183-4 (pbk.)

All photographs courtesy of Sharon Petty,
Mike Conklin, and Tom Bonen.

Copyright © 1981 by Ed Zolna and Mike Conklin
All rights reserved
Published by Contemporary Books, Inc.
180 North Michigan Avenue, Chicago, Illinois 60601
Manufactured in the United States of America
Library of Congress Catalog Card Number: 80-70639
International Standard Book Number: 0-8092-7184-2 (cloth)
                                    0-8092-7183-4 (paper)

Published simultaneously in Canada by
Beaverbooks, Ltd.
150 Lesmill Road
Don Mills, Ontario M3B 2T5
Canada

Contents

Foreword

Putting this book together has been fun. It isn't often someone who plays the sport so much can combine efforts with someone who has written so much about it.

No project of this nature would be possible without help from many persons and organizations. Those who have been especially generous with their time, effort, or materials include: Tom Bonen, photographer and founder of Windy City Softball; Diane Conklin, diligent typist; Bill Plummer III, public relations director for the Amateur Softball Association; the Connecticut Falcons professional team; the *Chicago Tribune*; Doug Bean, sportswriter; Ed Kirner and Aurora Home Savings; and the *Fox Valley Sports Journal*.

Ed Zolna and Mike Conklin

1
Getting Organized

One of my fondest memories in softball is of the time my team won both a Chicago city park championship and the Illinois Parks and Recreation state tournament on the same day.

This was possible because each of the events required a 20-man roster, which we submitted in full. There was no conflict until the final day of the tournaments—a Saturday—in which we were scheduled to play at approximately the same time at different locations, twenty miles apart.

In the morning, we split our roster in half and sent 10 players to the fields. The state tournament ended at noon and the players from this event then jumped into their cars and joined the rest of us at the city tournament.

By the time we were at full strength later in the day, my team already had won sev-eral games with the same 10 players. After we were united again, the second title was a breeze.

To the knowledge of the tournament officers, this was the only time a team had won both championships, since the events traditionally were held at the same time of the year.

The reason for mentioning this feat is not to boast of the accomplishments of my team, but rather to point out that through proper organization many things are possible. And although it is not an easy task to organize properly, make no mistake about it: There is no substitute in softball for being organized.

The best teams, no matter what the level, are those that have their acts together. Some may have better talent and others may have fancier pregame warmups, but it is those teams that are better prepared that typically emerge the most successful.

Superior organization begins with a take-charge manager who, in many cases, also is a player. It is the manager who lines up necessary basics such as players, equipment, and a schedule before proceeding to the sport's finer, more subtle details which separate winners from losers.

Unfortunately, many people think putting together a winning softball club is merely a matter of finding the best players available. It always has been my feeling that nothing could be further from the truth. In fact, talent, when it comes to players, is third on my list of priorities.

Here are the factors that go into a soundly organized softball team:

PLAYERS

The most important ingredient for a player has to be his or her attitude.

Playing softball with a serious-minded team is a big commitment, considering the length of a season which typically lasts three to four months and the number of games played within a week. This means players have to be very dedicated because there is generally no material compensation in amateur ranks and the hours spent on the field rival those put in on a full-time job.

The second most important item when it comes to players is availability.

It is one thing to want to play softball, but it does the team no good when other commitments get in a player's way and he or she can make only a portion of the schedule. There will be unavoidable conflicts, to be sure, but it is wise to have every potential member of your team look ahead

Being elected into the Amateur Softball Association's Hall of Fame in Oklahoma City is the ultimate honor for the sport's great players.

to his or her calendar for the entire campaign. If there are going to be major problems, don't let the association with the team go any farther.

The third most important ingredient is talent.

There are many things to be considered when judging a player's ability and, in most cases, the least important is his or her reputation. An athlete may have been an outstanding football or baseball player at some time, or perhaps was great at some other form of softball (fast pitch vs. slow pitch), but that doesn't mean he or she will be good at your game. It is always a good idea to personally check out new players either through preseason tryouts, practice games, or by scouting their performances with other teams.

The manager should not stand pat after settling on a basic squad. It is his job to continually improve the product; one of the biggest mistakes many managers make is to maintain the status quo each season with the same unit—while other teams pass them by.

It has been my practice over the years to add at least 2 new players each summer, which means that, after a decade or so, my team has undergone almost a complete transformation. Sometimes working new players into the lineup may mean you lose a few games early in the campaign, but in the long run it is a worthwhile practice.

It is the infusion of the new players, whenever possible, that creates depth for a softball team. I always try to play an extra player or two each game. This is a good way to keep everyone happy as well as have experienced performers on hand.

But, a warning: Never have a particularly large squad of 15 or so on hand for games. In the end, it isn't likely everyone will see action, and over the course of a few weeks this may cause dissension.

NONPLAYING PERSONNEL

Ideally, the manager should not be a player.

Cliff Smith (left), manager of the highly successful Aurora Home Savings fast-pitch teams, goes over a lineup with pitching great Charlie Sterkel.

In addition to giving him or her a broader viewpoint by being on the sidelines, it is also a good way to avoid any question of conflict of interest when selecting a starting lineup. On most softball teams, however, the manager also competes on the field because, in many cases, he or she is simply better than anyone else at a particular position.

Whenever possible, a player-manager is well advised to have an assistant on the sidelines who can point out details that might otherwise be overlooked. Another person who can serve a very useful role is the scorekeeper, whose statistics often provide a winning edge. Sometimes this person can be given extra responsibilities, such as arranging transportation for road games, checking for rainouts, and calling results in to the press.

A local gymnasium usually provides enough space for a workout, sans hitting.

PRACTICE

The amount of time a team practices depends upon its schedule. The more games you play, the less time you need to practice.

A team that plays only once a week should try to get in at least one other work-out during the week, but when there are at least two or three games per week—forget it. When a player is spending that much time with the team, it is usually too much to ask a part-time, amateur athlete to put in more hours.

The best way for a fast start in a new season is to get in some practice sessions before the opening game. If the weather is inclement, try to locate a gymnasium or fieldhouse where it's possible at least to play catch, loosen up with exercises, and take some swings with the bat.

The preseason practices do not have to be particularly sophisticated. Concentrate on the basics, especially hitting, and this alone should give you an edge at the start of a season. Many teams are rusty in the beginning, and the quickest way to gain momentum is through overpowering them with strong batting. The fielding should fall into place with more experience.

It is always nice to have big turnouts for practices. But it isn't always necessary to have a full complement. Just a handful of athletes means there still can be batting practice; in many cases, the sharpening of timing at the plate can be the most useful way a player can improve his or her worth to a team.

Before each game, it is advisable to have players show up as early as possible—especially if there has been no practice on an off-day. These pregame workouts should be tightly organized to cover a variety of items in a short period of time. For instance, while each player is taking five or ten cuts at the plate, another player can be hitting grounders and fly balls to the fielders.

The best idea is to jump on the vacant diamond as soon as possible and get in as much work as you can before the start of the contest.

TEAM SPIRIT

A player often is more effective when he or

she can simply concentrate on the game. It always has been the practice of our teams to build peace of mind through a variety of off-the-field activities. These range from having babysitters watch the tots to arranging postgame family picnics to keep wives and husbands interested in the action. Win or lose, we always top a season with a party for everyone.

SPONSOR

It costs money to play in leagues and tournaments. The more of that cost that can be defrayed by a sponsor, the less the players will have to dig into their own pockets. Naturally, with many of the high-powered teams sponsored by large corporations, this is not a problem.

The most obvious place to find sponsors are the businesses frequented by the majority of your players—taverns, sporting goods shops, restaurants. However, don't overlook the obvious, such as the businesses where each of the players is regularly employed. In an election year, politicians often sponsor teams.

LOCAL RULES

Be aware of any special rules in your league governing such items as rosters, injuries, substitutions, leadoffs, field conditions, and forfeits. The sport of softball may be essentially the same from town to town, but often there is a variety of minor differences.

For instance, your team may play in two leagues, and in one there is a roster limit of 15 and in the other the limit is 20. Be sure to take advantage of the difference and have full squads.

Perhaps the most overlooked rules are those governing out-of-play boundaries on the sidelines. Usually it isn't until after a player has made a super effort to catch a foul ball that you find out from the umpire that the fielder was beyond the limits.

Check beforehand to find out what the local rules are, to avoid risking the dangers of chasing into trees or bushes or tripping over equipment or benches in a wasted pursuit of a ball.

SCHEDULING

Scheduling is no problem for the better teams with experienced players. They've had the benefit of knowing at what level they're capable of playing. But if you're just getting started with a team, don't overextend it and try to play over your head in a tough group.

Schedule extra opponents when you think you're ready, as the season progresses. It's also always a good idea to get involved with

The circulation of your team's schedule before the season begins is the best way to avoid conflicts, such as a wedding set for the same day as a big game.

a postseason tournament that can serve as a goal during the regular season. Also, make sure every player has a copy of the schedule, and don't let any players leave a game without informing them of the time and location for the next contest.

ROSTERS

It is a good idea to turn in a full roster to league commissioners. Everyone may not play, and some of the names may be bogus, but it's a lot easier to bring in new players under old names on an 18-man roster that's full than it is when there are only 10 or 12 listed—and everyone else in the league knows who they are.

SANCTIONING

Be aware of the various governing bodies—*i.e.,* Amateur Softball Association, International Softball Congress—and their rules, especially if you're interested in postseason competition.

It can be very frustrating to have a team develop into a strong unit and then not get a chance to prove it further in a tournament because the manager forgot to register.

Sanctioning usually is done on a league or park basis, but double-check with other managers to make sure.

There's no question that this team's efforts have paid off with a victory.

Some softball in the off-season can help build strong ties among teammates.

Ty Stoflett, the dominant pitcher in U.S. men's fast-pitch softball in the 1970s. Stoflett was the key player on the first team from the United States to compete in the Pan-American Games and is a six-time MVP in the ASA national tournament.

2
Pitching

The pitcher, no matter what type of softball is being played and no matter what the skill level, is the hub of a game. A team's success almost always rises and falls with this person's ability to control his or her pitches.

Every play of a contest starts with the pitcher's underhanded delivery to the plate; how, where, and when the ball is served to the batter each time ultimately sets the tone for the entire match. It is no coincidence that this player is labeled No. 1 by scorekeepers.

As important as the pitcher is, however, there is wide variance in the objectives and rules governing his or her movements in the three major types of softball played: fast-pitch, 12-inch slow-pitch, and 16-inch slow-pitch.

Generally, the pitcher in fast-pitch softball is in a position to be especially domi-

nant because of the higher speeds at which the ball can be thrown. In many cases, the hitters simply do not make contact; they strike out, thereby relieving the defensive burdens of the pitcher's teammates.

On the other hand, the pitcher in slow-pitch faces a different ball game, since almost every hitter is able to make contact. Here, it is the goal of the pitcher to exert as much influence as possible on the batted ball.

The Amateur Softball Association, the sport's largest governing body, has different rules controlling the pitchers in the three different types of games. Here are some of the basic rules covering the movements in each one.

FAST-PITCH

The pitcher shall take a position with both

Joan Joyce, the dominant pitcher in women's fast-pitch softball in the 1960s and '70s. Joyce helped launch the Women's Professional Softball League and starred for the Connecticut Falcons following a brilliant amateur career with the Raybestos Brakettes.

No pitcher has dominated a national slow-pitch tournament like Ed Zolna, whose Bobcats won ten ASA championships.

feet firmly on the ground and in contact with the rubber.

Before pitching, the pitcher must come to a full and complete stop facing the batter with the shoulders in line with first and third base, and with the ball held in both hands in front of the body.

The pitch starts when one hand is taken off the ball or the pitcher makes any motion that is part of the windup. In the act of delivering the ball, the pitcher shall not take more than one step, which must be forward, toward the batter, and simultaneous with delivery of the ball to the batter. The pivot foot must remain in contact with the rubber until the other foot with which the pitcher steps toward home plate has touched the ground.

The release of the ball and the follow-through of the hand and wrist must be forward past the straight line of the body. The hand shall be below the hip and the wrist not farther from the body than the elbow. The pitch is completed with a step toward the batter.

The pitcher may use any windup desired, providing: he or she does not make any motion to pitch without immediately delivering the ball to the batter; he or she does not use a rocker motion in which, after having the ball in both hands in pitching position, he or she removes one hand from the ball, takes a backward and forward swing and returns the ball to both hands in front of the body; he or she does not use a windup in which there is a stop or reversal

In this fast-pitch warmup, the pivot foot stays in contact with the rubber as the weight is transferred, and the ball is on its way.

of the forward motion; he or she does not make more than one revolution in the windmill motion; he or she does not continue to wind up after taking the forward step, which is simultaneous with delivery of the ball.

12-INCH SLOW-PITCH

Here again, the pitcher must come to a complete pause before starting the pitch.

Any windup may be used here, too, but the ball must be released at a moderate speed—a speed left entirely up to the judgment of the umpire.

The pivot foot must stay in contact with the rubber until the pitch leaves the hand.

The ball must be delivered with a perceptible arch of at least three feet from the time it leaves the pitcher's hand until it reaches home plate. The ball shall not reach a height of more than 12 feet at its highest point (although unlimited arch is used in many leagues).

The pitcher may use any windup, providing: he or she does not make any motion to pitch without immediately delivering the ball to the batter; the windup is a continuous motion; he or she does not use a windup in which there is a stop or reversal of the forward motion; he or she delivers the ball toward home plate on the first forward swing of the pitching arm past the hip.

16-INCH SLOW-PITCH

Once again, the pitcher must come to a complete pause before starting the pitch and the pivot foot must stay in contact with the rubber until the ball leaves the hand.

The speeds of the ball and arch are the same as 12-inch slow-pitch, as are the rules governing windups and deliveries. However, the pitcher may use two hesitation pitches if he or she desires before the mandatory delivery.

The distance between the pitching rubber and home plate is 38 feet instead of 46 in fast-pitch and in 12-inch slow-pitch (40 for women in fast-pitch).

The pitcher may attempt to pick a runner off since leadoffs (but no steals) are allowed.

SLOW-PITCH OBJECTIVES

The batter can make contact with the softball almost at will in slow-pitch, but it would be a mistake to think that this means the pitcher's role is minimal. In effect, it is just as important as in fast-pitch because he

A slow-pitch pitcher in 16-inch ball is about to launch a delivery.

This pitcher has "jammed" the batter with an inside pitch.

or she is the only person who can influence whatever success the hitter enjoys.

The slow-pitch pitcher exerts control over the batter in the same manner as the pitcher in any other brand of softball or baseball: by knowing the hitters and throwing to their strengths and weaknesses. Because there is no way to simply overpower the person at the plate, the pitcher in this game should be even more alert than in the others.

The slow-pitch pitcher's most effective weapon is the arch.

The higher it is, the slower the speed of the ball heading for the plate and the more difficult for the hitter to make contact with a level swing because of its angle. The lower the arch, the faster the ball is traveling and the easier it is to control. While this may make the pitch a better target for a level swing, it also makes it possible to directly counter the batter's strength by pitching away from it or overloading the defense.

For instance, a right-handed batter has been pulling the ball all day. An inside pitch

with a low arch will virtually guarantee another ball stroked to left field into a defense readied for the expected result. Or, a low outside delivery with a low arch makes it difficult for this batter to pull the ball.

It is especially helpful for the pitcher and catcher to work together, noting what the other team's players have done at the plate in previous trips and adjusting pitches accordingly. Before long, certain theories begin to become obvious.

Some examples:

The batter with the wide stance, gripping the end of the bat, is particularly vulnerable to the high pitch.

The batter who consistently hits grounders also has trouble with high pitches.

The batter with a closed stance and choked bat usually finds it difficult to hit low pitches.

The batter who consistently hits fly balls also has trouble with low pitches.

There are several other keys to becoming a successful pitcher in slow-pitch softball. They include:

Vary the height and speed of pitches. Just as it becomes possible for a baseball player to dig in on a pitcher who continues to groove deliveries, the same can happen in softball.

Work out a system of complete signals to the fielders that indicate where you plan to throw a ball. This, in turn, gives them an idea of how to play the pitch.

Note as soon as possible in a game how the umpire is calling pitches. Unlike fast-pitch, there tends to be a wide variance in slow-pitch of how umps call strikes and balls and it is to the pitcher's benefit to have this knowledge.

In 16-inch, use your hesitations to full advantage. Mix up the number you use, stay consistent for a while, and then mix them up again at varying speeds. The idea is to keep the hitter off-balance.

Check the wind. A good breeze gives you an excellent way to curve the ball.

Be aware of lights during night games and the sun in day games. Many times it is helpful to deliver the ball in a manner in which the hitter has trouble picking it out of the sky—just as the lights and sun can be a problem for fielders catching flies.

This slow-pitch pitcher is in the process of putting plenty of spin on the ball.

Get set to field after each pitch. Many times, the pitcher may wish to consider jumping several yards back after the delivery to serve as an extra fielder.

Do not try to catch every grounder up the middle. If it's to the right or left, remember that you are backed by a second baseman and a shortstop.

Practice an effective throw to the bases on balls that you field. After throwing dozens of underhanded pitches, a pitcher sometimes finds it awkward to suddenly have to throw with an overhand motion.

Vary the spins on pitches. Practice being able to throw a ball with the back of the hand facing the plate and releasing it with an upward flip, a motion that puts considerable spin on the ball. Mix it up with a floater that spins very little. Many batters become confused when they see something a little different coming from the pitcher—and a split second of confusion or indecision can mean the difference between an easy pop fly and a line-drive single.

Be particularly aware of what bases should be backed up. The action unfolds very quickly in slow-pitch, and not being in the right defensive position to stop an overthrow can cost a run.

Alter the starting spot on the rubber. It gives the hitter something else to think about.

Whenever jumping way ahead of the batter with an 0-2 or 1-2 count, try for a pitch with an extremely high arch. The batter has to be guarding the plate, and there's no telling (for him or her) whether that ball coming from the clouds just may cross the strike zone.

The pitcher's stride off the rubber doesn't necessarily have to be directly toward home plate. Work at making it a diagonal step, therefore being able to throw the ball at a more severe angle.

FAST-PITCH OBJECTIVES

Obviously, this pitcher is in position to dominate a game with no restrictions on the

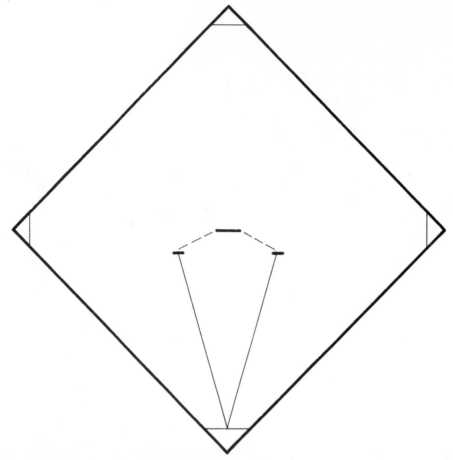

This chart illustrates the different angles a ball can travel to the plate if the pitcher takes a diagonal step instead of one straight at the plate.

speed of the delivery. As a result, many of the top performers, who record between 10 and 18 strikeouts per seven-inning game, also develop an impressive arsenal that includes fastballs, curves, drops, and rises—although good speed is enough against many hitters.

The fast-pitch pitcher usually operates from two basic deliveries: windmill and slingshot. The purpose of either is to get the full power of the body, arm, and legs behind every pitch. The best pitchers are just as likely to use one as the other, but it is a good idea to concentrate on a specific motion early in a career.

Windmill

In this delivery, the softball travels through almost a complete circle as the arm is swung up and around before the pitch is completed.

Starting from the basic stance with both feet touching the rubber and the softball gripped by the glove and nongloved hand, swing both arms forward and upward without straining. At the same time, shift your weight over to the foot on the side of the pitching arm.

From this position, pull the ball out of the glove as the pitching arm continues swinging upward. By now, the left foot (for a right-handed pitcher) lifts off the rubber and starts moving forward to help maintain balance. The arm continues up and back with the weight still on the right foot and moving toward home plate.

The throwing arm now begins to straighten and the wrist cocks back as the downward swing begins to gather momentum. The left foot also completes its glide toward the plate, and the weight begins to shift

A pitcher at three key stages of the windmill delivery in fast-pitch softball.

onto the left foot as you push forward with your right.

All of this begins to create a whipping-arm action with the added power of legs and body as you thrust your weight forward against the braced leg. Just before the release, the upper part of the body is turning to face home plate with the wrist still cocked back for the final power snap which whips the ball from the hand.

Following the release, the motion should continue with a full follow-through. All the weight is on the left foot, but the right foot swings forward with a natural motion. Both feet should finish almost even, with weight evenly distributed for fielding purposes.

Slingshot

In this motion, the ball travels back and up to a layback position, then whips down and forward. It starts with the same basic opening position, with weight evenly balanced, feet in contact with the rubber, and the ball clutched between both hands.

Shift the weight to the right foot (for a right-handed pitcher), pivoting the body to the right so the left shoulder faces the plate. The left foot then rises off the ground to begin a stride toward the plate. As the pitching arm begins swinging back, the wrist is bent loosely forward. At the top of the backswing, the wrist bends back into a cocked position. The backward reach should be as far as possible while still feeling comfortable.

By this time, the stride toward the plate has been completed with the weight still concentrated on the back foot. As the arm is whipped downward, your weight pushes forward onto the left foot and the body begins to pivot toward the plate. The wrist is cocked back and the hand turned out slightly at the wrist, with the wrist no farther from the body than the elbow. The critical part, however, is that the snap of the wrist must come as the ball reaches the release point, and you continue pushing the weight forward onto the left foot.

As the wrist snap and whipping motion is completed, all your weight and power has been put behind the pitch. In the follow-through, let the right foot swing forward into a comfortable position with weight balanced evenly on both feet to allow better fielding.

It is important to work at consistency, reaching the same point in the layback position on each windup and timing the release for the same spot.

The fast-pitch pitcher, because of the speed he or she is able to generate, has at his or her disposal a greater variety of pitches. In fact, it is possible to do more with a softball pitch than a baseball pitch because of the ball's size.

For instance, with plenty of hard work, not only can the fast-pitch pitcher master a fastball, change-up, curve, and drop, but he or she also may find it relatively easy to develop an effective riseball.

Riseball

Just as it sounds, this pitch perceptibly rises from the time it leaves the pitcher's underhand motion and arrives at home plate.

This rise is above and beyond the normal trajectory of the delivery. It is caused by the pitcher's ability to put a backspin on the ball so that the ball, in turn, takes an upward cut.

The riseball is a hard pitch to master because first the player must be able to throw the softball with exceptional velocity. When this stage is reached, the actual grip is thus: the ball is held with the palm facing forward, the little finger and thumb pointed upward, and the forefinger pressed against a lacing after being tucked backward.

Upon delivery (from either a windmill or slingshot), the back of the knuckles is aimed toward the plate; as the ball is delivered, the forefinger pushes sharply to deliver a backspin.

This pitch requires considerable work because the pitching hand assumes what will be, at first, an uncomfortable grip. However, the riseball is a dangerous weapon

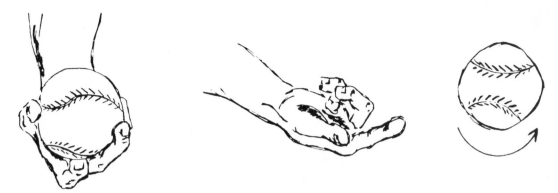

Here is the typical grip in throwing a riseball. Note that the forefinger is tucked.

Here is the grip commonly used for throwing a drop ball. The ball is rolled off the fingertips when delivered.

against a batter who is forced to make a last split-second adjustment. The trick, like a baseball player throwing a curve, is not to hang the pitch. It should start in the strike zone and finish above it, thereby forcing the hitter—if he or she makes contact—to strike a bad pitch.

Drop Ball (Sinker)

This is an equally dangerous weapon that is considered by many fast-pitch pitchers to be easier to throw than the riseball. Therefore, it usually is thrown more than other types of trick pitches, and good hitters are more likely to make adjustment because of their familiarity with it.

The pitch does exactly what it says. The drop, or sinking motion, is more than the normal trajectory of a delivery.

The idea is to put extra, forward roll on the softball as it leaves the hand; it won't seem too difficult because of the underhanded motion. The ball should be gripped with the palm up, thumb on the outside, and two fingers cradling it underneath. It is

then released on the upswing so that it will roll off the middle fingers, creating a top spin which will produce the downward dip.

Curve

The danger with this pitch is that it is not as easy to attain a downward trajectory as it is in baseball, where the pitcher is throwing from an elevated mound. In softball, the pitcher is on the same level as the batter, and the curve isn't as hard to hit because it usually maintains the same plane.

A good curve should be used in much the same manner as the riseball. Ideally, it should start as a strike and finish outside the strike zone by the time it reaches the plate, thereby forcing the committed hitter to make contact with a bad pitch.

Nevertheless, the pitcher starts out by using the same grip that he or she employs for throwing a straight fastball. The curving motion comes from a twist of the wrist, either inward or outward, that is given at the moment of release. This movement produces extra spin in the direction the ball is traveling and this rotation, in turn, makes the ball curve.

A right-handed pitcher, for example, makes the softball curve farther to the right by rolling the ball off the thumb and forefinger while twisting the wrist in a clockwise direction. If the ball is to curve in the other direction, the wrist is snapped in a counterclockwise direction and the ball is released with all four fingers starting to come over the top at the moment of release.

Change-up

Without question, the change-up can be the most effective delivery in a fast-pitch pitcher's arsenal. The batter must always be prepared for fastballs because of the lightning speeds involved and this, in turn, means it is nearly impossible to adjust to a ball coming in at a radically slower speed than is expected.

If the batter is able to make contact, more than likely it will result in a harmless pop-up or weak grounder to an infielder.

There is no standard motion or grip for the change-up, but it is important that the pitch is not tipped in advance because batters will pounce with relish at something arriving at the plate with a manageable speed. Therefore, it is typical for the good pitcher to disguise his or her change-up with a windup and delivery closely resembling that of another pitch—only to slow the speed of the hand and arm at the last possible moment.

Signals

It is especially important for the pitcher and catcher to work out a set of signals. They do not necessarily have to be the standard numerals flashed by the catcher with his or her fingers as is the custom in baseball. They can be merely a tap on the leg, tip of the mask, or shift of the catcher's glove.

But, it is extremely important for the catcher to know what pitches are being delivered; his or her job—catching the ball—is almost as difficult as the batter's, since he or she is facing the same pitches. Additionally, in many tight, closely played fast-pitch games, a passed ball by the catcher can mean the difference in the outcome.

3
Hitting

Hitting is where it begins for many in softball. If a team can't hit, rarely is it going to win games because it won't score enough runs.

Hitting in slow-pitch softball is considerably different than in fast-pitch softball or baseball, where the same basic fundamentals are followed. One of the biggest mistakes batters make is to employ the same techniques at the plate that are used in all bat-and-ball games.

The differences, obviously, center on the speed of the ball.

The ball comes to the plate much faster in baseball and in fast-pitch softball and, therefore, elements such as quick reflexes, eyesight, strength, and aggressiveness become vital. The primary goal is to make contact with the pitch in the most efficient manner possible.

It's almost impossible not to make contact in slow-pitch softball because the ball comes to the plate at such a leisurely pace; therefore, the techniques and styles employed by a batter change with priorities. Elements such as selectivity of pitches, bat control, and footwork become more important. In short, there is considerably more finesse involved, and this requires sound understanding and mastering of fundamentals.

STANCE
The rigid, taut, usually compact positioning by the batter at the plate in baseball and fast-pitch softball isn't as necessary in slow-pitch softball because the hitter has more time to make adjustments before the ball arrives.

It is important, however, to follow the

This hitter shows excellent form as he is about to unleash his swing.

basic principles of keeping elbows away from the body to ensure a smoother cut, to stride in a manner that forces streamlined transition of weight from the back foot to the front foot, and to time the swing in a fashion that creates contact at the precise moment and level desired.

There can be less emphasis in slow-pitch softball on where the bat should be positioned before the swing starts, but it is still necessary to concentrate on footwork as it plays a vital role in which direction the ball will travel—an important weapon in a team's hitting attack.

The three basic patterns are: closed stance, where the front foot is placed closer to the plate which allows for easier opposite-field hitting; square stance, where both feet are parallel to an imaginary line drawn from the plate to the pitching rubber; and open stance, where the front foot is stationed farther from the plate than the rear foot. The distance feet are planted apart usually varies from 12 inches to a yard.

Many times the team on the field will observe where the batters place their feet to help determine in which field the ball will be hit, but it is possible in slow-pitch softball to take advantage of this trait and confuse the opposition with a quick, last-second shift, since there is ample time before the ball arrives.

SELECTIVITY

One of the most difficult parts of batting,

especially for the newcomer to slow-pitch softball, is selectivity of balls to hit.

There is a real temptation for the rookie, mainly those making the shift from baseball or fast-pitch, to pounce on every delivery. The pitches all look very inviting as they hang in the air, heading plateward.

It's always a good idea to take the first pitch if for no other reason than to get a better line on how the umpire is calling them.

The successful batters take plenty of time in practice to carefully note what pitches they hit most successfully. They also note the results of how they handle balls that are low, high, inside, outside, and how well they hit the varying arches. A hitter should always look for what he or she likes best at the plate, but knowing the other possibilities opens new options for the various situations that occur in a contest.

The key to selecting the right pitch is to have patience; one of the worst things a batter can do is to make up his or her mind beforehand as to whether he or she will take a cut. Many times it is more obvious to a base coach or an on-deck batter that a ball will be high or low, and they have enough time to inform the person at the plate before the pitch arrives.

SWING

The swing starts with the wrists cocked and, as it develops, the arms become fully extended at the time of contact before the wrists roll over on the follow-through.

While this is taking place, the weight that formerly was on the back foot is transferred to the front foot. At the time of contact with the ball, the front leg generally is straight and the rear leg bent.

The timing of the swing is very important. Pop-ups, grounders, and other unhelpful results often are the product—in addition to swinging at bad pitches—of a swing that isn't properly coordinated with the stride, shifting of weight, or extension of the arms.

A left-handed batter demonstrates a perfect follow-through at the plate.

Oftentimes, the hitter can cure bad timing by going to a heavier or lighter bat.

There is no percentage in trying to muscle the ball. The good hitter works at perfecting a smooth, steady swing to be used in most situations and then speeds it up or slows it down when the situation calls for a harder or softer stroked ball.

There are many ways the batter can strike the ball with his or her swing, and it is not a cardinal rule to attempt to hit the ball squarely in the middle. For one thing, it must be remembered in slow-pitch that the ball is coming to the plate from an angle, and the swing has to be aimed in a manner that takes this fact into consideration.

Choking up on the bat is the same in all bat-and-ball games. By doing it, the hitter can easily increase bat speed but he or she usually sacrifices a little power in the process.

WHERE TO HIT

"Hit it where they ain't" is a famous baseball expression that is just as applicable in softball.

It may seem more difficult in slow-pitch because of the extra fielder, but this is balanced by the fact that the hitter can exercise more control over accuracy due to the slowness of the pitches. This means there are more things that can be done to the ball, such as striking the bottom half for backspin, connecting on the top half to create top spin, or cutting it on the side to create a curling effect.

The good hitter generally looks for several types of pitches that he or she prefers and then tries to master hitting the ball to certain areas on the field that are unguarded.

Many baseball practices, such as hitting grounders behind the baserunners or going for long flies with runners in scoring position with less than two outs, are just as viable in softball. Many batters like to shoot for the baselines since this almost always means an extra base hit, but with two strikes and foul-ball limitations in effect, the smart batter then tries to go up the middle.

TIPS

Everyone has his own ideas of how to be a good hitter. Some aren't conventional, but if they work, keep at it. The experienced players pick up many tips during their careers. Here are ten that may be helpful:

- If you're striking too many fly balls against a low-arch pitcher, consider using a shorter stance, try a heavier bat, aim for striking the ball slightly above center, or wait longer before starting to swing.
- If you're hitting too many ground balls against a high arch pitcher, try choking up on the bat, use a lighter bat, aim to hit the ball slightly below center, or work at utilizing a quicker swing.
- In order to hit the ball harder, try either a short run before the swing (making sure not to step out of the batter's box) or employ a slight movement backward with the arms and bat just before beginning to swing.
- Keep your eye on the middle of the pitched ball.
- Conjure up a mental picture of where you're going to hit the ball before stepping to the plate.
- Unless a specific situation dictates otherwise, always try to cross up the fielders by doing the opposite of what they expect.
- Control the tempo of the pitcher's deliveries by occasionally stepping out of the batter's box or asking for time out.
- Be patient.
- At least once every outing, whether in batting practice or in the game, make an attempt at hitting the ball to the opposite field.
- Go with the pitch and don't try to power the ball to a specific spot if the delivery isn't conducive to that.

This slow-pitch hitter (top left) will take a short run at the ball in an attempt to generate more power.

This batter (top right) shows good concentration as he is about to make contact with the ball.

The on-deck hitter (bottom right) frequently is in excellent position to yell instructions to a homeward-bound teammate.

The base coach should give clear signals to the runners.

4
Baserunning

Running the bases in softball is something that requires more concentration and alertness than it does in baseball. The bases are considerably shorter in softball. This means that the extra base is closer for the opportunist.

Many rules concerning this part of softball have changed in recent years, but baserunning has remained important because it often is the difference between two teams in a close game. It's been my observation that, given teams of equal ability in hitting, pitching, and defense, the club with the better baserunners—and that doesn't necessarily mean the fastest—will win 80 percent of the time.

A key element of baserunning always has been the base coaches. This is one of the few areas where players can get aid while the action unfolds, and everyone should take full advantage of this.

Many managers just pick volunteers to coach, usually opting for a reserve or someone batting late in the order. It really doesn't make any difference who gets the jobs at first and third, but it is a good idea that there be consistency.

The coaches need to develop a rapport with runners, who want to know how, when, and where to expect instructions while circling the bases. They have to be just as involved with how the game is unfolding as the rest of the players. A mistake by this person usually means an out and the loss of a possible run.

The two coaches are of equal importance. A mistake by the person at first base may mean there will be no one for his counterpart to help at third.

The runners should start looking for instructions as soon as they leave the batter's box. If the ball is on the ground and it looks

The alert base runner should look for instructions as soon as possible.

The base runner who puts extra effort to work can make a difference in a game.

as if a close play is in store at first base, the coach at first should point at the bag as a signal for the runner to give it all he or she has got to beat the throw. If the coach wants the runner to circle the base to be alert for possible advancement to second, he gives a circling motion. If the runner is going to be good for at least a double, it's a "go" signal all the way.

The third-base coach has to be particularly demonstrative and decisive because in this situation the runner's eyes are almost always away from the play. A turn to see what's happening results in the loss of at least a step, which can mean the difference in a game.

Generally, when in 12-inch slow-pitch games, try to squeeze that extra base out of a hit because the bases are farther apart and there is no leading off. Therefore, sometimes it is more difficult to get runners in scoring position.

Sliding is an extremely significant part of good baserunning. The two reasons for sliding are to prevent the tag for an out and to avoid injury through a collision.

There are three basic types of slides.

The most common variety is the straight-in slide, where the top leg is kept nearly straight and the bottom leg is bent at the knee. As contact is made with the bag, the runner can use the base as a fulcrum to rise quickly and be alert for the next move.

The fall-away, or hook, slide is more difficult to execute but extremely helpful in evading what may appear to be a sure tag by a fielder. In this case, the body is thrown away from the base either to the inside or outside and then the bag is hooked with whatever foot is on the nearest side.

The third slide is the head-first slide, which is rarely used. The advantage here is that the runner is directly facing the play

This base runner starts his straight-in slide.

and can see clearly which way to put his or her hand on the bag to avoid a tag. The bad part about this slide is that, for some, it takes more time to get back on the feet to be ready for another dash. The slider also is vulnerable to face injuries.

The key to any of these slides is to start the move at the appropriate time. Too soon, and you may never reach the bag. Too late, and you risk injury by crashing into the base while providing a bigger target for the fielder.

It's important to be alert when running the bases on a batted ball because in softball the other opportunities to steal are not as prevalent as in baseball. In the first place, it's illegal to steal in slow-pitch and almost impossible in fast-pitch because of the great speeds of the pitches.

Although it is illegal to steal bases on a pitch in slow-pitch ball, there are some significant differences in the rules in 12-inch and 16-inch competition.

This base runner saw an opening through the catcher and used a straight-in slide to safely reach home plate.

Base runners are not allowed to lead off in 12-inch softball and, therefore, the most helpful advice for the person on base is to be braced and ready to go at the crack of the bat.

In 16-inch slow-pitch, where the bases are 55 feet apart compared to 60 in 12-inch games, leadoffs are allowed. However, base runners cannot advance on pickoff attempts and those pitchers who are especially skillful often have perfected crafty plays to nab runners.

Sometimes, no slide at all is the best way to avoid a tag.

Overrunning a base often leads to embarrassing situations.

A base runner applies the brakes after rounding second base.

5
Infield Defense

Rarely does a team win games without a solid infield defense.

Whether it's fast-pitch softball, where the majority of hits are grounders, or slow-pitch softball, where batters hit almost any pitch at will, it is almost impossible to be successful without consistently making flawless infield plays.

The cornerstone for a solid infield defense is the fielder's ability to catch a ball hit on the ground and throw out runners. The snaring of line drives and flies is important, but it is grounders that will be hit most of the time to the infield.

The fielding of ground balls can be broken into two parts: catching the ball, and the throw. And while quick reflexes are important, it is possible to become proficient through hard work.

Here is a breakdown of the fundamentals involved:

FIELDING

The basic position is for the glove to be near the ground just inside the front foot. Keep low, close to the ground, with your rear almost in a squatting position, and let the ball roll into the glove.

It is always easier to rise up for the ball that takes a high bounce than it is to drop quickly for the ball that stays low. In turn, ground balls should always be caught in a glove coming in an upward motion rather than downward as this also facilitates a better throw.

The fielder should be ready on each pitch by assuming a crouched position to make it easier to start the play. There can be variations, depending on a player's comfort, but the feet should be spread, knees bent, weight slightly forward, and eyes on the ball from the moment it leaves the pitcher's hand.

A second baseman shows flawless form in fielding a grounder.

While spotting her target, this infielder gets the proper grip on the ball.

A third baseman is ready for anything that comes her way.

It is best to try to get planted squarely in front of the ball for a cleaner pickup while always seeking to play the ball on the bounce you prefer. Never take your eye away to see what is happening to the runners.

After the ball is in the glove, the motion for the throw begins.

THE THROW

With the softball tucked away, the fielder looks at his or her target and, at the same time, begins to feel for the proper grip on the ball when taking it from the glove. The ball, glove, and throwing hand are all touching at this point and they continue in a motion that is backward and upward. The stride toward the target also is started with the front foot aimed at the proper base.

The goal is for the entire motion to become one smooth, continuous flow of action that takes as little time as possible. A sidearm or overhand toss is optional, but the fielder should use the same one all the time and it should be of the variety that yields maximum accuracy and swiftness.

On some plays, an infielder doesn't have enough time to use any of the standard throws, and an underhand toss will have to be employed.

Each infield position has distinctive responsibilities. Here is a breakdown:

CATCHER

In slow-pitch softball, this probably is the best spot to put the weakest fielder. The rare instances when the catcher is part of the action, aside from receiving the pitcher's normal deliveries, are catching fly balls, fielding slow rolling grounders, and tagging

A catcher demonstrates one of the job's chief responsibilities—blocking the plate.

a base runner trying to score. In each case, this person can be aided by another fielder: a pitcher or first baseman can cover the plate for a putout; a pitcher, first baseman, or third baseman can field the slow rollers; or any infielder within range can snare the pop flies.

The slow-pitch catcher doesn't have the equipment found in baseball and fast-pitch softball and, on close plays at home, it is essential for this person to work at applying quick tags on hard-charging runners with a minimum of body contact. The best way is to get set either behind home plate or to one side of the baseline, touching the runner as he or she passes.

The catcher is in excellent position to be a team's defensive quarterback, since he or she has a clear view of plays as they unfold and typically is not directly involved. This is the person who can shout instructions to cutoff fielders on relay throws or help on high flies that are being surrounded by more than one fielder.

A catcher needs to make sure on a tag play that the ball is low enough that the base runner can't avoid contact by sliding under it.

A first baseman in 16-inch slow-pitch shows why it doesn't hurt to be tall.

Also, the catcher is in an excellent spot to help with the positioning of fielders according to a hitter's strengths and weaknesses. On wide-open fields and when there is no one on base, the catcher may want to follow the runner to first base on infield grounders to back up the play.

PITCHER

More and more, softball teams are realizing the potential for this position on defense—especially in slow-pitch. A few backward or sideward steps following the release of a pitch and the pitcher is an extra fielder.

However, one of the most common mistakes a pitcher makes as a fielder is his or her attempt to catch every ball. Often, the play can be more successfully turned by another fielder. The difficult catch attempted by the pitcher might have been easier for a teammate.

Also, a pitcher should work at his or her tosses to other bases after catching grounders or flies. The reason? After making dozens of underhanded deliveries, the pitcher may find it uncomfortable to suddenly make an overhanded toss.

FIRST BASEMAN

The first baseman generally is one of the tallest players on a team, making it easier for him to catch throws from teammates—this player's chief chore.

Getting to the base to receive the throw is the trickiest part of the job. The first baseman usually wants to play as far from the bag as possible without being so far that it is difficult to get back in time to be set for the throw. The most common practice is to anchor one foot on the inside of the bag, and then, without committing oneself too soon, use the other leg to stretch toward the throw to cut down on the time needed to catch the ball.

If keeping the foot on the base would mean missing the catch, take the necessary steps to make the catch. It is better to catch the ball and miss the putout than to miss the putout and have the ball sail away and give the runner extra bases.

Above all, never plant the foot on the outside of the bag and provide an obstacle for the runner.

Since there is no bunting in slow-pitch (the first baseman usually plays in front of the bag in fast-pitch for this reason) the first baseman should stay behind the bag for

A first baseman's stretch for the ball can mean the difference between a single and an out.

Using two hands is a necessity for a first baseman in 16-inch slow-pitch softball.

possible grounders. Obviously, if it is a left-handed batter, he or she should play a little deeper and closer to the foul line.

The first baseman also is in an excellent position to start double plays. But, if it means there won't be enough time to get back to the bag for the throw, it may be better to run to his or her base for the first out and take a chance on the second runner having to be tagged at second base, since the force out will have been removed.

The first baseman also is a key person on relay throws to home plate from the outfield and, typically, he or she is the cutoff person on those balls hit to right field. However, this player should remain in the infield on these plays.

SECOND BASEMAN

This player gets the benefit of usually having the shortest throw to first base and he or she therefore can be a little more relaxed in getting off the toss. On the other hand, this player also faces many different duties and he or she should be among the quickest of the infielders.

For instance, the second baseman during the course of a game may have to cover second base on double plays; cover the bag on throws from the outfield; cover first on slow, short choppers fielded by the first baseman; back up throws from the outfield; and cover second on steals.

Oftentimes the second baseman has to range far to his or her left or right to field a grounder, requiring an off-balance throw. It is important to try and get a foot planted before making the toss.

The second baseman should spend considerable time working on double plays, one of the most disheartening occurrences in the game for a team at bat. Never toss the ball to a teammate covering the bag if the play can be just as easily started by tagging the base yourself. If a throw is required to someone covering the bag, make it eye or shoulder high.

An infielder needs to be alert for the runner who slides past the base.

SHORTSTOP

Because this is a tough position to play, generally the job should be handled by one of a team's better athletes.

For one thing, the shortstop has to have an exceptionally strong and accurate arm since his or her throws are the longest to be made among the infielders. In addition, often the throws have to be made off-balance after grabbing balls hit to one side. It is just as important for this player to know when not to throw as it is to know when to throw. Don't throw if there's no chance. It just creates an opportunity for an error.

With no one on base, the shortstop generally plays deeper, to allow more room to field grounders. He or she also becomes a relay person on hits to left field and a pivot person on cutoff plays, and must stay alert for covering second base on possible double plays.

It is important for the shortstop, as well as the second baseman, to touch the bag on double plays as quickly as possible and then move to one side to make the throw to first

base. However, in 16-inch slow-pitch this job frequently is handled by the short center fielder.

THIRD BASEMAN

The third baseman needs to have quick reflexes since he or she is closest to the plate of all the infielders (with the exception of

This second baseman made the tag before the runner could break up the play.

the catcher and sometimes the pitcher), and has little time to react to a batted ball. However, even though it is a long throw to first, this player has the advantage of extra time, since the ball arrives quicker.

The third baseman has to be ready at all times because of the closeness to the plate; he or she should begin each pitch low to the ground with feet braced and glove poised.

In slow-pitch, the third baseman always should be alert to guarding the foul lines (like the first baseman) in certain situations because balls stroked close to the line usually mean extra-base hits.

Two tips: Be sure to note the terrain in foul territory in order to avoid crashing into any trees, fences, scoreboards, dugouts, etc., in pursuit of flies. Also, stay alert to the location of base runners since the snaring of hot liners frequently can be turned into double plays.

A good infielder is able to make the spring upward to handle high-bouncing balls.

An infielder's tagging of a base runner is helped considerably when the ball arrives in plenty of time.

An outfielder sometimes has to make an extra effort when he has misjudged a fly.

6
Outfield Defense

There is a tendency among inexperienced softball managers to overlook the importance of the outfield. How many times does the novice manager, in making out a lineup, stick the weakest players in the role of the outfielder? Unfortunately, it happens too often.

Instead, playing the outfield should be regarded as one of softball's most important jobs. In slow-pitch, where batters can wallop the ball long distances almost at will, the outfield is one of the game's busiest locations. In fast-pitch, where pitchers dominate and most of the outs are strikeouts or grounders, the outfield is a key spot because an error can easily lead to a run in the typically low-scoring contests.

No matter what the game, there are certain fundamentals to be followed by outfielders.

FLY BALLS

Playing the outfield starts with being able to catch fly balls. If you can't, find another position.

Naturally, the key to catching flies is related more to being able to tell where the ball is going rather than the actual physical process of gathering in the ball. If you're in the right spot, the catch should take care of itself.

There are many factors that can enter into the judgment surrounding flies, including wind, sun, lights, field conditions, teammates, pitching, and trajectory of the ball. Almost all can be mastered through practice; no outfielder should ever enter a game without having shagged a few flies.

The most important part of making the catch is getting a jump on the ball—which translates into a timely start—in order to be in the right spot. This allows the maximum amount of time to get set for the catch. In other words, anticipation.

It helps if the outfielder is playing in the right spot before the pitch is even delivered. Obviously, the left fielder should be a little deeper for the right-handed power hitter, the right fielder should be a little deeper for the left-handed power hitter, etc. More on that later.

Of course, every ball usually isn't hit precisely to the outfielder. Therefore, he or she should position the feet in a defensive stance that allows a quick turn in either direction. Also, many fielders prefer to stand in a spot a step or two deep before the pitch, figuring that it is always easier to make up the distance coming forward for a shallow hit than it is to drop back for the deeper blow.

For most outfielders, going back for the long, deep fly ball is the most difficult trick. Never run backward, a sure way to trip and land on your backside. Instead, pick the location where you think the softball will land, run straight to that spot, and turn in the direction that will allow the quickest reaction for the catch.

If there is a wind of any consequence, the outfielder should alter his or her actions on the long fly by making the backward turn in the direction that the breezes are blowing. This is because the softball will have a tendency to drift away from the fielder in the direction of the wind.

If the fielder is able to get underneath the ball in good order and the play calls for a quick throw following the catch, he or she will want to help the toss by positioning the foot of the side of the body they throw from slightly behind the other foot. This will facilitate getting a stronger start for the toss to the infield.

The catch itself can be done in several ways, providing it is not made on the run. There is the simple, one-handed catch with the glove waiting for the ball, basket-style, with palm upward. Or, there is the more standard catch with the glove and palm facing away from the body.

If the outfielder seeks a little insurance, the two-handed catch is advisable—especially for the inexperienced player. If it is to be a basket catch, the little fingers of the glove and nonglove hand should be touching. If it is to be the more standard, palm-upward grab, the thumbs of the glove and nonglove hand should be touching.

If the play calls for a quick throw, a one-handed, palm-upward catch is the best, since it allows for the throwing arm to be in a closer position for the throw.

Above all, it is a cardinal rule to let your hands give a little as the ball drops into the glove. This movement serves as a shock absorber and usually prevents the ball from bouncing out of your hands.

GROUND BALLS

The fundamentals for fielding a ground ball in the outfield are basically the same as those observed by infielders regarding positioning of the feet and glove.

The basic difference, however, revolves around the distance between the fielder and runners. Whereas the infielder almost always has a chance to throw out the batter after fielding a grounder, the outfielder rarely has that opportunity.

The outfielder has more time to catch the ground ball because of this distance, meaning the ball is traveling at a slower speed than it is in the infield. The outfielder thus is able to have extra moments to line up the softball for a easier bounce or even to go down to one knee to make sure the ball is blocked.

The outfielder then should not hesitate in getting the softball to the proper cutoff player, as the bases are closer to each other in softball than they are in baseball, making it easier for the aggressive runner to stretch the single into a double or the double into a triple. Of course, any ball with some steam that gets past an outfielder can easily be turned into a home run.

The key to effectively fielding the ground ball by the outfielder is making sure to get low enough for the catch. This should entail getting the rump down almost into a squatting position and then watching the softball travel right into the glove. The most common way a fielder lets the ball get through him or her is by taking the eye away from it, trying to see what the runners are doing.

POSITIONING

There is no problem concerning where outfielders locate themselves in fast-pitch softball; there are only three of them and the general procedures used in baseball are followed. Typically, however, the outfielders play a little shallower than in other games because of the pitcher's ability to overpower batters.

However, in slow-pitch softball it is a different game because there is a fourth fielder. In 12-inch ball, the standard procedure is to play the four fielders straight across—one each in left, left center, right center, and right. The left and right fielders have the option of playing closer to the foul lines to protect against dangerous hits that land just inside fair territory and can be turned into extra bases. There also is the possibility of the left center or right center fielder playing shallow when he or she is in the opposite field for the hitter, thereby choking off a high-percentage area. Sometimes this fielder comes in all the way to second base to help out in relay situations.

In 16-inch ball, where it is more difficult to hit the ball longer distances, the extra fielder typically is brought in to play directly behind second base to guard against the frequent line drives up the middle. Also, since the bases are shorter, this player is in a position to act as a second baseman on double plays and force outs. This, in turn, takes pressure off the shortstop and second baseman and increases their range by relieving them of the burden of covering the base.

Since pitchers frequently back up to serve as a fielder following their deliveries, the extra outfielder—or short center fielder, as he or she is called in 16-inch softball—is usually well-advised to play a few yards behind second base.

The smart teams move their extra fielder around, trying different depths and locations relative to the strengths of the hitter and the game situations.

TIPS

A softball player learns many shortcuts and other helpful ways to play the game. This is especially true in playing the outfield. Here are some tips that should prove useful:

• Don't Duplicate. When a ball is stroked between two outfielders, the two defensive players should not copy each other's actions, with both trying to run it down. The slower fielder should give way to the faster teammate, then assume another responsibility such as moving to back up the play or going to a cutoff spot for a possible throw.

• Know Your Territory. An outfielder should always check out his or her turf, especially when on a new field. Softball games generally are not played on the plushiest layouts, and locating gopher holes, large rocks, and other obstacles is a good way to prevent sprained ankles or more serious injuries. Also, check for markers such as warning tracks, trees, foul poles, or whatever can be used to tell your location.

• Help Your Teammate. Many times a fellow outfielder can be helpful by calling out warnings, footage, or other helpful items to a teammate. Fielders should check signals beforehand to avoid any confusion.

• Throw on a Line. The throws from the outfield should be made hard and low even if it means they bounce before getting to the infielders or cutoff person. The defense has no control or options with balls that are thrown high in the air; such balls can allow runners precious seconds to steal an extra base. Know ahead of time where you will be throwing.

• Playing the Sun, Lights. The key to not losing sight of the ball is following its flight

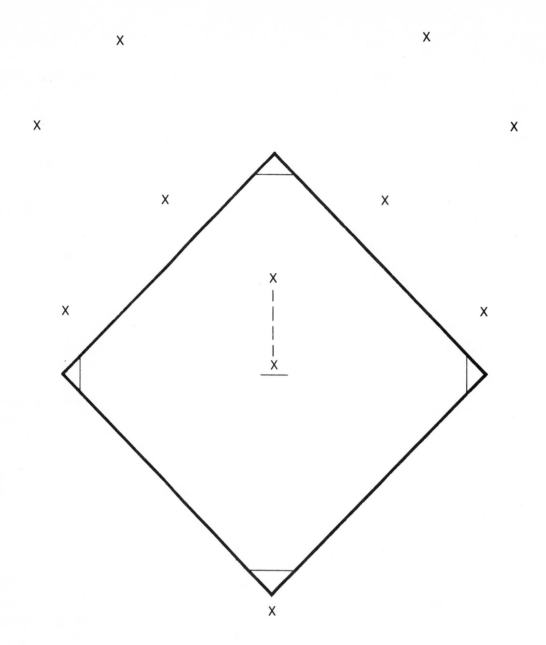

from the moment it leaves the pitcher's hand. Once it is lost in the sun or lights, don't panic and look away. Instead, try to judge where you think it is headed and pick up the flight there. Always try to keep the eyes shaded if it appears there will be a problem, but another good idea is to take a single step either to the left or right to get a different angle on the ball.

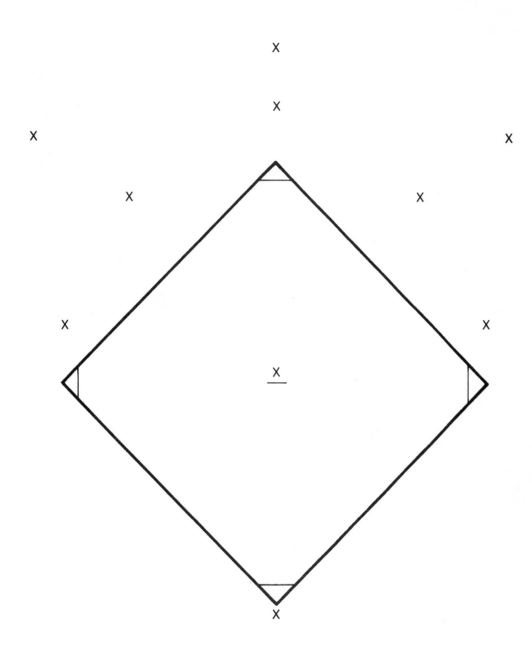

The typical alignment in a 12-inch slow-pitch game is four players in the outfield (see p. 40). Often in 16-inch slow pitch, the extra fielder is moved to a spot directly behind second base (above).

Mundy Team Statistics—22 Games   Record: 18–4

HITTING

PLAYER	G	AB	R	H	BB	2B	3B	HR	RBI	LOB	Avg.
Klein	21	79	33	41	5	8	0	2	22	25	.519
Reilly	21	81	26	41	2	10	3	4	35	17	.506
Cella	18	69	27	33	6	5	0	2	21	3	.478
Valenta	9	32	9	15	0	2	0	2	9	5	.469
Zale	11	39	11	18	5	4	0	1	12	5	.462
Santos	10	40	13	18	1	5	1	2	19	4	.450
Kamowski	16	54	23	22	9	3	0	1	13	5	.407
Conklin	9	27	8	10	2	1	0	1	8	8	.370
Rivers	20	74	19	27	5	8	0	5	18	18	.365
Katz	7	23	6	9	4	2	0	0	4	5	.365
Courtney	16	58	13	21	3	3	0	0	10	13	.362
Gantner	20	68	16	24	8	3	0	0	8	8	.353
Edes	9	32	8	9	2	0	0	0	3	10	.281
Bogira	14	38	13	10	15	2	0	0	9	12	.263
Zwerling	11	35	5	9	2	1	0	1	5	11	.257

FIELDING

OUTFIELD	Chances	Assists	Putouts	Errors	Pct.
Cella	30	3	24	3	.900
Klein	63	2	54	7	.889
Kamowski	32	2	22	8	.750
Rivers	22	4	10	7	.682
Zale	13	1	10	2	.845
Valenta	10	0	9	1	.900
Santos	13	1	9	3	.770
Katz	4	0	3	1	.750
INFIELD					
Reilly	59	24	28	7	.882
Gantner	86	23	50	13	.849
Zwerling	43	23	12	8	.812
Rivers	37	18	8	11	.703
Edes	43	0	41	2	.954
Bogira	24	0	24	0	1.000
Courtney	19	0	19	0	1.000
Santos	6	1	5	0	1.000
Conklin	2	0	1	1	.500
PITCHERS					
Cella	21	16	4	1	.952
Bogira	15	11	3	1	.934
Conklin	3	2	0	1	.667

PITCHING

	G	IP	R	ER	H	BB	K	W–L	ERA
Bogira	13	85	89	59	129	30	4	10–2	6.36
Cella	7	38.6	74	38	85	18	8	7–0	3.23
Conklin	3	20.3	38	23	45	13	0	1–2	7.91

A team's up-to-date statistics provide a great deal of information to the manager.

7 Statistics

There is an expression in sports that statistics are for losers, but it's always been my contention that statistics can turn you into a winner. There are several ways this can be done.

The most obvious is through a careful compilation of individual and team accomplishments during games. This, in turn, provides a handy index for finding strengths and weaknesses as the season progresses.

One of the most important nonplaying members of a team should be the statistician. The records he or she keeps can be broken down into three categories: hitting, fielding, and pitching.

All statistician's records should be kept in a Stat Book, which is updated religiously following every game to allow quick reference.

In the book, one page lists the name of every player and next to each name are columns for the number of games played, at bats, runs, hits, doubles, triples, home runs, runs batted in (RBI), walks (including how many were intentional), strikeouts, sacrifices, number of double plays hit into, stolen bases (fast-pitch) times caught stealing (fast-pitch), errors, and how many times hit by a pitch (fast pitch).

A separate page is kept for pitching statistics in which after the name of the pitchers there are columns for keeping track of won-lost records, earned run average, number of games appeared, games started, complete games, innings pitched, hits allowed, earned runs, walks allowed, strikeouts, wild pitches (in fast-pitch), hit batsmen (also fast-pitch), home runs allowed, and saves.

Some record keeping goes beyond just the individual totals of each player and the totals for the squad as a whole. For example, some record books contain the score sheets from each game in chronological order. This allows a check on which batters, fielders, and pitchers have been especially productive in recent games. Hence, adjustments and shifts can be made to provide maximum firepower in lineups.

But some go even further than this.

Because some teams play more than a hundred games a season, and many of those are against the same teams, it may be helpful to keep individual sheets on each player for an even more telling reference. Here, it can be the practice to record each player's performance in every game on a separate line in which, in addition to the statistics already noted, the opponent, opposing pitcher, date, weather conditions, and any other noteworthy fact can be recorded.

This additional information gives the softball manager an added perspective for judging his players' capabilities. For instance, Bill Smith may have only 10 hits in 20 games as indicated by a quick glance at the team sheet. However, a closer check on his individual sheet reveals that eight of his hits came in three games in which he faced pitcher Tom Parker, today's opposing hurler. Obviously, even though Smith's overall average isn't so hot, he has to be given extra consideration as a starter when going against Parker.

This practice is not limited to hitters.

Individual files are kept on pitchers, where on each line the date of every appearance, opponent, hits allowed, walks, runs, earned runs, strikeouts, innings, decision, home runs, location of contest, and any noteworthy performances by opposing batters (two hits or more, extra-base hits, good contact) are noted.

Even armed with all these statistics, some scorekeepers go one more step and jot down any other facts from a game that (they think) may be beneficial in a future contest. This can include the umpires and what type of pitches they tend to favor, opposing play-ers who rattle easily or have rabbit ears, defensive shortcomings of the opposition, field and weather conditions, and habits of the other team's top hitters.

Of course, it is one thing to gather all this data and another to put it to use. Too many times managers hurt themselves by not surveying their statistics—something which should be done before every game—to find the strongest possible combinations for an opponent.

It isn't enough just to rely on your memory or to go with what has been your strongest lineup in recent games. Statistics can provide the winning edge.

A team's statistician should know how to figure batting averages, slugging percentages, earned-run averages, fielding percentages, etc.

BATTING AVERAGE

Divide the number of times a hitter has been to bat officially (excluding walks, sacrifices) into the number of hits he or she has produced. Carry your math out to three decimal points. For instance, if a player has been to bat 80 times and has 20 hits, the average will figure to .250.

SLUGGING PERCENTAGE

To find this statistic, divide a player's total official times at bat into the total bases made on all of his or her hits—remembering that a batter gets one total base for a single, two for a double, three for a triple, and four for a home run.

ON-BASE PERCENTAGE

This is determined by taking a player's total appearances at the plate (including walks, sacrifices) and dividing it into the times he or she has been on base (except for a fielder's choice or error). To get the player's on-base total, add the hits, walks, number of times reached base on interference, and number of times hit by a pitch (fast-pitch). Then, divide this total by the total appearances at the plate.

FIELDING AVERAGE

To find this all-important average, divide the number of chances a fielder faces with the number of chances accepted (total number of putouts and assists).

EARNED-RUN AVERAGE

This is determined on the basis of a seven-inning game (standard length for softball matches) for the pitcher. Multiply the pitcher's total of earned runs by seven and divide that result by the number of innings pitched. Round off thirds of an inning.

8
Scoring

One of the real unsung heroes on a softball team can be the scorer.

Unfortunately, the job of scorekeeping usually is relegated at the last second to a different person at each game, such as a player not in the lineup, a relative, or a fan. Sometimes the job is transferred during the action.

Instead, whenever possible, the responsibility should be given to the same person at each contest in order to develop a uniform scoring system with game-to-game continuity.

The scorekeeper, of course, is the hub for all the team's statistical gathering.

During the course of a game this person can be as significant as any competitor on the field. There have been numerous times when the scorer has helped batters stay alert to the game by keeping everyone informed, and therefore attentive, about the hitting order. In addition, there will be many times when he or she keeps the opposition "honest" by making sure their lineup doesn't undergo any strange substitutions or the order doesn't get jumbled.

In addition, in games that become especially high scoring, which frequently occurs in slow-pitch, the scorekeeper becomes particularly vital in keeping the many runs straight.

Scorebooks can be purchased in just about any sporting goods store; each page typically will have space for a dozen names or so down one column, followed by columns representing the innings. The name lines for the players intersect with the column for each inning, providing a space for showing what the batter did at his or her turn at the plate. This is shown in the form of a diamond—representing the bases—within a square.

Actually, there are a number of ways to keep score in softball, and no two persons go about it the same way. However, there are certain basics almost everyone follows, and the differences in styles tend to be minor, individualistic variances to cover special circumstances.

Scorekeeping is your link with what's taken place on the field during and after the contest, and one of the most important principles is that this chronicling of the action can be read and understood at any time—whether it's immediately afterward or a month later. It is a shortcut for writing everything down in longhand.

There are a variety of symbols, abbreviations, and numbers to be used in recording what the batter does at the plate. Conversely, they also serve to record the achievements of the defense, since details of the putouts also will be indicated.

To begin with, each defensive position is given a number. The pitcher is 1; catcher, 2; first baseman, 3; second baseman, 4; third baseman, 5; shortstop, 6; left fielder, 7; center fielder, 8; and right fielder, 9. The extra fielder used in slow-pitch is 10.

If a batter hits a grounder to the third baseman and the third baseman throws to the first baseman for the out, this is recorded simply as 5-3 in the scorebook under the appropriate inning. A fly out to the left fielder is F-7.

If a base runner on first is thrown out by the catcher attempting to steal second, and the second baseman takes the throw and applies the tag, it is 2-4. If the situation is a double play with the third baseman throwing to the shortstop covering second and then on to the first baseman, it is 5-6-3.

In short, every defensive player who touches the ball on an out—even if it is a deflection—should be recorded.

What if a batter reaches base?

Well, if it's a hit, a line is drawn on the appropriate diamond in the scorebook and it is extended to the base reached by the batter. Then, if it is a single, a single slash mark is drawn perpendicular to the line—or sometimes a scorer may be more emphatic and write in 1b. If it's a double, a line is filled in to second base and either two perpendicular slashes or 2b is written. If a batter reaches base on an error, a line is drawn to the appropriate base and an E, followed by the number of the errant fielder, is written.

The scorekeeper continues to chart the progress of the batter who's reached base and, if he or she eventually scores, it is a good idea to fill in the encircled diamond to make it easier to add up runs.

There are a number of symbols used to record common occurrences. They include BB for a walk, SB for a stolen base, HBP for a hit batsman, DP for a double play (with the play further indicated by the appropriate numbers), SAC for a sacrifice out, and K for a strikeout (a backward K is used when the batter fails to swing at the third strike).

In addition, a scorer many times will add his or her own markings to give further details, such as where a hit was made or the count on the batter when he or she advanced to an out or base.

One special note. It is always a good idea to promptly record totals at the conclusion of each inning so there can be no problems with attributing RBIs (runs batted in), stolen bases, hits, and other important details, which sometimes can get lost in the postgame shuffle.

RUPERT'S _____ VS. _____ MUNDY'S _____ AT _____ EVANSTON _____ DATE 7-21-79

PLAYER	Pos	AB	R	H	PO	A	E	TB	2BI	SB
Zale	6	3	2	1	2	3	0	1	0	0
Rivers	8	4	1	1	2	0	0	1	1	0
Reilly	5	4	2	3	1	2	0	4	0	0
Valenta	9	4	2	4	3	0	0	10	6	0
Klein	7	3	0	0	1	0	1	0	1	0
Bogira	3	2	0	0	7	0	1	0	0	0
Edes	4	4	0	0	0	2	0	0	0	0
Kamowski	10	3	0	0	1	0	0	0	0	0
Santos	2	3	1	2	3	0	0	3	0	0
Cella	1	3	1	1	0	1	1	0	0	0
TOTALS		33	9	12	21	7	3	20	8	0

2 base hits ... VALENTA, REILLY, SANTOS
3 base hits ... VALENTA
Home runs ... VALENTA
Double plays ... 2 (REILLY-BOGIRA), (CELLA-BOGIRA)
Triple plays ...
Bases on balls off ... CELLA 2
Struck out by ... CELLA 3
Earned runs off ... CELLA 4
Opponents' hits off ... CELLA 8
Wild pitches ...
Passed balls ...
Left on bases ... 7
Winning pitcher ... CELLA
Losing pitcher ... ZWERLING
Umpires ... KATZ, COURTNEY
Time of game ... 1:15
Scorer ... M.C.

This score sheet shows much about Rupert's team effort against the Mundy's. For instance, note that Valenta had an especially good day with a single, double, triple, and home run. Note that Santos, the catcher, had three putouts. On the other hand, Kamowski had a bad day by striking out twice, once without swinging at the third strike.

9
Softball Today

You don't have to be a detective to discover how popular softball is in the United States.

Drive through just about any portion of rural America on a warm, summer evening and it won't be long before you come across a community with the lights above the local ballfield burning bright. Stroll through the huge parks of the nation's largest cities in the late afternoon or early evening and you're sure to come across a game.

Reliable estimates place the figure at 35 million for persons playing some sort of softball in 52 countries. The bulk of the competition takes place in the United States, but you're just as likely to find games in London's Hyde Park, in mainland China, or in New Zealand. Every four years a world championship tournament for fast-pitch teams is held.

More than 27 million Americans now participate in softball—making it America's most popular team sport.

The Amateur Softball Association, which has almost two million registered members and approximately 80,000 teams worldwide, is the sport's largest sanctioning body. The ASA also conducts the largest network of national tournaments in the United States. This network includes divisions for 15 groups in fast- and slow-pitch for men, women, and youths. Approximately 80 percent of those who play are on slow-pitch teams.

There have been many reasons forwarded as to why the sport is so popular; perhaps that in itself—the fact that there are many reasons—is ultimately the best commentary. It is good recreation within a structured framework that can be as competitive as an individual wants. The sport knows no ethnic

51

Softball teams line up for pretournament ceremonies at a recent ASA national tournament.

barriers and, considering the large number of house leagues involving institutions such as churches, schools, fraternal organizations, and other segments of society, it is an outlet that can be as much social as competitive.

The ASA is much more than just a conductor of national tournaments and a rules dispenser. The association also is the springboard for affiliates such as the International Softball Federation, National Federation of Umpires, National Scorekeepers Association, and the National Association of Softball Writers and Broadcasters. In addition, the ASA publishes a monthly magazine and a yearbook.

One of the ASA's proudest achievements is the construction of its Hall of Fame in Oklahoma City, where the national headquarters is located. Hall of Famers have been selected by the organization since 1957, but it wasn't until 1977 that the doors of a permanent new home were opened.

The ASA is not the only sanctioning body for softball, which branches into schools and professionalism.

The International Softball Congress (ISC), headquartered in Greeley, Colorado, is an organization for fast-pitch teams; it has been around in one form or another since 1947. The ISC stages an annual tournament; and the Long Beach Nitehawks, one of the many western teams in the organization, dominated the event in the 1970s and has fared well against the ASA champions in that time.

The ISC is the outgrowth of the National Softball Congress which, at the time it was started in 1947, was more interested in women's softball. In the fall of 1950, a group of men interested only in fast-pitch formed the ISC at a meeting in Chicago.

Among the many displays at the ASA Hall of Fame in Oklahoma City are copies of all the organization's guide books dating to 1933. These machines give the visitor an opportunity to test his or her knowledge of the game's rules.

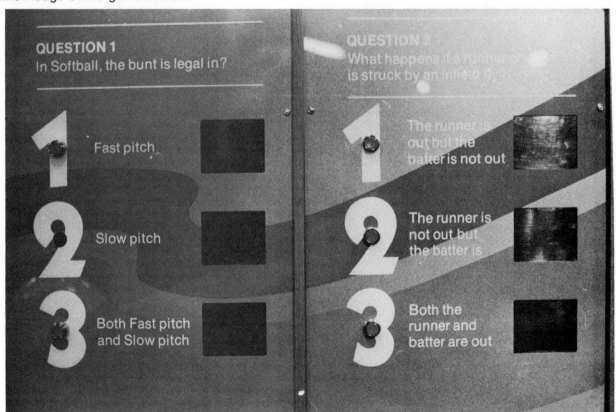

The first tournament was held the next year in Greeley, Colorado. This group's Hall of Fame, established in 1965, is in Long Beach, California.

The U.S. Slow-pitch Softball Association (USSSA) is another sanctioning body that has been spurred by the recent fast development of slow-pitch ball. The group, started in 1967, already is the second largest body in the sport, with approximately 4,000 registered teams.

Members of Nelson's Painting Service team celebrate after capturing the 1977 Men's Major 12-inch slow-pitch championship in Parma, Ohio.

It was the USSSA that in 1975 triggered one of the sport's most important developments with an antitrust suit against the ASA. An out-of-court settlement had the significant effect of making it possible for teams to have dual memberships and for those in each organization to play against each other, something that had been forbidden in previous seasons.

Softball today also has made some giant strides in schools, particularly among women athletes.

The National Federation of State High School Associations reports there are close to 6,900 schools in the U.S. that regularly field women's fast-pitch teams, involving about 165,000 athletes. There are just under 1,000 schools that have women's slow-pitch teams, with 20,000 girls as participants.

For the high school boys, there are close to 175 softball teams for both slow- and fast-pitch, with about 3,200 athletes.

The high school programs are the foundation for growing involvement in softball—especially for women—at the college level.

The ASA first sponsored a College World Series for women's fast-pitch teams; now the Association of Intercollegiate Athletics for Women has taken over the administration of the annual championship tournaments, which are conducted for both slow- and fast-pitch teams in three categories based on sizes of schools and amount of money spent on respective programs.

The future for college softball for women, spurred by the enactment of Title IX federal legislation that has elevated girls' scholastic programs through availability of more money, is bright. The sport has come from practically nowhere to rank as the AIAW's number 4 activity in terms of participation by member institutions.

All of this leads to another side of softball—the pros.

There have been several attempts at forming professional fast-pitch leagues for both men and women, and each attempt has failed. The latest and best publicized was the International Women's Professional Softball Association for fast-pitch teams, which opened for business in 1976 and shut down after the 1979 season. The league was dominated by Joan Joyce, the best woman pitcher in the history of the game.

Softball touches all walks of life. In Chicago, one of the game's biggest boosters is Pulitzer Prize-winning newspaper columnist Mike Royko, a devotee of the Windy City style of ball without gloves.

Still alive are the newly organized North American Softball League and the American Professional Slow-Pitch League, both slow-pitch leagues for men. The APSPL opened in 1977, and the NASL got started in 1980.

George Halas, founder of the National Football League and owner of the Chicago Bears, has remained a softball enthusiast dating from the days in the 1920s when he used the sport as a conditioner for his football players.

10
Softball Yesterday

Chicagoans always have had special feelings about softball, the Windy City's most popular outdoor summer activity. Chicago is the birthplace of softball. In addition, two other important developments occurred there: Chicago was the site of the first national championship, and the site for the founding of the Amateur Softball Association, the game's largest governing body.

It all began in 1887 in Chicago's fashionable Farragut Boat Club on Thanksgiving Day, when a group of Harvard and Yale alums were awaiting the result of the annual football game between their schools (Yale won 17-8). One of the men picked up a boxing glove and started tossing it around to other Farragut members, who began batting it around with a broomstick.

Before long, George W. Hancock, a Chicago Board of Trade reporter, devised a set of informal indoor rules similar to those of baseball—a sport undergoing rapid growth in the United States at the time. Hancock and his friends marked out lines on the floor with chalk, marked bases on a wrestling mat, and knocked the "ball" around to the tune of 41-40. The rules were put on paper, and the indoor game continued to be a popular pastime that winter for Farragut members.

The next big city to embrace a version of softball was Minneapolis, where Lt. Lewis Rober of Fire Company No. 11 introduced the game in 1895. It was a recreational outlet for restless firemen and was played in a vacant lot next to his firehouse. A field approximately half the size of a baseball diamond was marked out with a pitching distance of 35 feet.

Eventually Rober was transferred to

another company, and he took the game with him. Other firehouses also started playing; before long there were leagues and a city-wide tournament, attracting crowds of approximately 3,000.

One of the big problems in early years was a name for the new game.

In Minneapolis, it was called Kitten Ball in honor of the nickname of the first fire department team. But as the sport began spreading to other parts of the nation, park district and assorted recreational officials called it everything from Mush Ball and Pumpkin Ball to Big Ball and Twilight Ball.

Finally, the name softball was introduced by Walter Hakanson of the Denver, Colorado, YMCA in 1926 at an organizational meeting in Chicago. The name stuck.

The confusion over the name in the formative years wasn't nearly as chaotic as the confusion over rules of the game. The distances for the bases and pitching rubbers differed from city to city and state to state, as a variety of organizations—YMCAs, playground associations, athletic clubs, etc.—got into the act.

The first interstate group that tried to get everything straightened out was the National Diamond Ball Association. That group was started in 1925 by Harold A. Johnson, who put together his own set of rules after an exhaustive study of how the game was played in neighboring areas.

Johnson's organization—which sponsored a season-ending tournament—grew to include nearly a thousand teams in the upper Midwest. The 1932 tournament expanded to include forty teams from six states.

It was in 1933, however, that the sport got its biggest shot in the arm with the formation of the Amateur Softball Association and the organization of a truly national tournament in conjunction with the Chicago World's Fair.

The Chicago tournament was the brainchild of the promotion department of the *Chicago American* newspaper, which was

The late Harold "Shifty" Gears of Rochester, New York, was the first person elected to the Amateur Softball Association's Hall of Fame. Gears, a pitcher, led Kodak Park to two national titles in 1936 and 1940, won 881 games, lost 115, threw 61 no-hitters, 373 shutouts, and struck out 13,244 batters during his career.

anxious to put together an event to match the athletic extravaganzas initiated by the rival *Chicago Tribune,* such as the All-Star baseball and College All-Star football games.

Chicago American sportswriter Leo Fischer came up with the idea for the softball tournament; the newspaper, part of the Hearst chain, dispatched him to scour the country for representative teams. With the help of other promoters, he eventually had enough solid entries for separate divisions for fast-pitch and slow-pitch for both men and women.

The *American* reported that 70,000 spectators attended the championship games.

The Chicago tournament officials gathered together after the competition to form the International Joint Rules Committee, a major step at standardizing the variety of rules many teams used before coming to town. It was from these meetings that the Amateur Softball Association was born and, with the help of $50,000 from the Hearst papers, the annual national meet became a fixture.

The late Marie Wadlow was the first woman named to softball's Hall of Fame. Wadlow, a pitcher, had a record of 341-51, threw 42 no-hitters, and played from 1929 to 1950.

Alberta Kohls Sims of Alexandria, Kentucky, was the first female slow-pitch player named to the Hall of Fame. An outfielder, Sims led teams to three national titles and was named an All-American four consecutive years (1961-64).

The ASA-sanctioned tournament continued to be played even through World War II, although it eventually was shifted from Chicago to Detroit before moving on to many different cities. The original tournament has grown to include divisions of competition for 15 or more groups of men, women, and youths.

Fast-pitch was the dominant style in the early days before peaking in the 1940s, when pitchers began dominating games. This stifled the action for players and fans alike. The situation was complicated further by the tendency among large companies that sponsored teams to recruit and stockpile top hurlers.

This helped further the cause of slow-pitch, a game that previously had been reserved mostly for old-timers and those not quick enough for fast-pitch. The first ASA men's slow-pitch national tournament finally was held in 1953, 20 years after the fast-pitch inaugural; the initial women's national meet came in 1962.

Members of the Fort Wayne, Indiana, Zollner Pistons (including sponsor Fred Zollner, over right shoulder of center player) celebrate the first of three consecutive national fast-pitch tournament championships in 1945. The Pistons are the only team to win three straight national fast-pitch titles.

11 Extra Bases

The complete softball person is not just someone who can hit, run, throw, and field. He or she is also a person who knows the game's rules, history, and other off-the-field aspects. This chapter is designed to cover many of these extra details.

PUBLICITY

It is no coincidence that some softball teams seem to get more newspaper space or TV and radio time than others. Stories and scores do not appear in the media by magic. It takes coordination and cooperation.

In some cases, it may be advisable to work through the host park district or league. Either way, at the start of the season check with local sportswriters and sports desks about how you can best serve their interests in trying to get publicity for your team.

More than likely, and depending on the size of the newspaper or other media outlet, you will be told to simply call in scores and be prepared to give a few details. Follow through.

It is through consistently following up on the suggestions of local sports editors and assignment desks that you will get your best publicity results. Don't think that *Sports Illustrated* is interested in your league championship, but when something important is coming up, such as a league showdown or tournament, draw the attention of the appropriate media to the event.

UNIFORMS

According to ASA regulations, all players on a team must wear uniforms that are identical in color, trim, and style. If this rule were enforced to its fullest extent, more than half the teams in the nation would be out of business.

However, outfitting a team isn't as expensive as it would seem, and it is a good idea for those players expecting to put in a lot of seasons to purchase uniforms—pants of a basic color that could be interchangeable with different tops.

There are three basic styles of uniform pants: knickers, similar to baseball togs; shorts; and the ankle-length, loose-fitting variety favored by many players of 16-inch slow-pitch.

Uniforms that feature shorts are favored by women's teams (above). This is what the well-dressed player (top right) with a knicker-style uniform looks like. The final player (right) exhibits the loose-look uniform.

EQUIPMENT CARE

The proper upkeep of equipment such as spikes and gloves helps prevent errors and, more importantly, injuries. An occasional linseed oil treatment, perhaps several times a summer, is an excellent way to keep gloves in good shape.

The 16-inch softball favored by most teams.

Kneepads sometimes are a welcome item for the softball player wearing short pants.

TROPHIES

Trophies, whether for team or for league accomplishments, are good for morale. Don't wait until the last second to purchase trophies; some comparative preseason shopping is one way to cut expenses.

GAME OF INCHES

What does it mean when someone refers to 16-inch or 12-inch ball? The measurements refer to the circumference of the ball. (A 12-inch ball is used for fast-pitch.) Stay tuned, though. Fourteen-inch slow-pitch is catching on in some parts of the country.

BASIC DIFFERENCES

There are some fundamental differences in the three major types of softball: fast-pitch, 12-inch slow-pitch, and 16-inch slow-pitch. They are easily confused.

Here is what players should know about their respective games:

The length of the base lines in fast-pitch and 12-inch slow-pitch is the same—60 feet. In 16-inch, it is 55 feet.

Aside from the speeds of the ball, there are some other basic pitching variances. The distance from the rubber to the plate in fast-pitch and 12-inch slow-pitch is 46 feet (40 for women). It is 38 feet in 16-inch. Also in 16-inch, the pitcher can make two hesitation deliveries before throwing the ball.

In baserunning, the runner is not allowed to leave the base in fast-pitch until the ball leaves the pitcher's hand—and then, stealing is allowed. In 12-inch slow-pitch, there is no stealing but the runner is allowed to leave a base after the ball reaches home plate. In 16-inch, there is no stealing but the runner is allowed to lead—but is not allowed to advance on an errant pickoff throw by the pitcher.

Bunting is allowed in fast-pitch, but is forbidden in all slow-pitch.

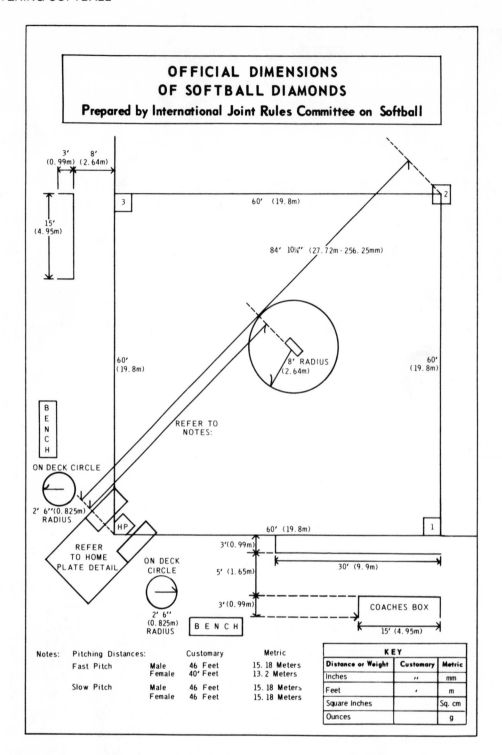

Here are the official dimensions for a softball diamond when a 12-inch ball is used and the players are adults. However, the base paths are 55 feet in 16-inch ball.

Bunting is legal only in fast-pitch softball.

The minimum distance for outfield fences in fast-pitch for men and women is 225 feet. In 12-inch slow-pitch, the distance must be 250 for women and 275 for men. In 16-inch slow-pitch, the distance must be 200 feet for women and 250 for men.

BATS

The official bat shall be round, made of one piece of hard wood, or formed from a block of wood consisting of two or more pieces of wood bonded together with an adhesive in such a way that the grain direction of all pieces is essentially parallel to the length of the bat. The bat shall be no more than 34 inches long and not more than 2¼ inches in diameter at its largest part. In its entirety, a bat shall not weigh more than 38 ounces. A bat shall be marked "Official Softball" by the manufacturer. Bats also may be made of metal.

PROTESTS

The notification of intent to protest must be made immediately before the next pitch, and it must be filed within a reasonable time. Protests that shall be received by the appropriate persons must concern the following matter: misinterpretation of a playing rule; failure of an umpire to apply the correct rule to a given situation; and failure to impose the correct penalty for a given violation.

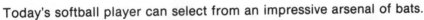

Today's softball player can select from an impressive arsenal of bats.

Svelte softball players (and umpires) sometimes are hard to find.

12 Conditioning and Practice

There is probably no aspect of softball that is more overrated than conditioning.

It is best to be in top overall physical condition to be a good softball player. However, this sport does not require the use of as many parts of the body as, say, a more demanding activity such as wrestling, swimming, or basketball.

Instead, softball is a game of specific movements and, in most cases, it is necessary for a player really to have to work at only four or five basic activities to improve performance. For instance, it is not important to have the running endurance of a miler or marathoner. Rather, it is only of value to be able to sprint as quickly as possible for less than 100 yards, while making sharp turns, to cover all the bases. In most cases, the sprint only goes from home plate to first base.

Aside from running, other basic physical elements of softball would include the ability to bend over quickly to catch ground balls or line drives; the strengthening of arms, back, and shoulders to make a swing of the bat more streamlined; or strengthening of the shoulder, arm, and wrist to aid the throwing of the ball.

With this in mind, it is not necessary for a team and manager to invest thousands of dollars in expensive weight equipment or other physical fitness programs to ensure success. Some simple conditioning exercises—some of them simulating game situations—should suffice.

Every player should know his or her capabilities and what degree of physical conditioning it takes to reach and maintain his or her best level. Although it is not necessary to be a superbly conditioned athlete to be a

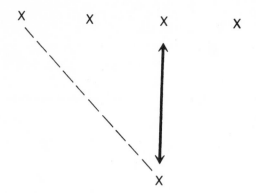

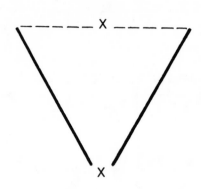

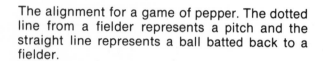

The alignment for a game of pepper. The dotted line from a fielder represents a pitch and the straight line represents a ball batted back to a fielder.

Diagram for a game of pickup, with the fielder moving laterally in both directions to make grabs of grounders thrown by a person in a stationary position.

good softball player, it is common sense to try getting into shape for your own general well-being. Furthermore, there is no question that staying in good condition is a solid way to avoid nuisance injuries such as muscle pulls and ankle sprains.

In effect, no season should be approached by a player without some form of preseason training if for no other reason than to simply sharpen concentration. Additionally, no game should be approached without some form of pregame workout for the same reason.

There are a number of ways to do this. Following is a list of a variety of conditioning drills and exercises that can be employed with or without teammates and with or without equipment. Some are good for outside use with plenty of room; some could be employed indoors.

Pepper

This is probably the oldest, best-known drill for softball players wanting to sharpen their fielding reflexes. It can be used with only two players, but typically four or five are best. The principle is simple. One person with a bat hits pitches thrown from other players forming a line 15 to 20 feet away. The idea is to swat sharp grounders and line drives to the fielders, who need to stay alert

to make the catches. This is an especially effective pregame warmup, giving infielders a chance to loosen up while the other team is on the field for pregame drills. It also can double as practice for the batter, who is able to sharpen his eye-hand coordination with the bat.

Bench Drill

Obviously, strong legs are an asset in softball because strength aids in adding speed for sprints to the bases. The building up of legs is something that can take place any time. This is a good exercise for improving strength. It is simple. All that is needed is a chair or bench that is 3 to 4 feet off the ground. The player jumps and places one foot on the bench while keeping his or her weight on the foot remaining on the floor. Another jump is made in which feet are exchanged by placing the opposite foot on the bench and floor. Ideally, this exercise should be repeated as quickly as possible, up to 50 times.

Weighted Bat

The use of a weighted bat is especially popular for hitters about to go to the plate during a game. The objective is to make the regular bat seem lighter, therefore easier to get around in time on a quick pitch. Obviously, the use of a weighted bat is more prevalent in fast-pitch softball. It is a good idea to have two or three weighted bats on hand for a team, and they should vary in size. If holes are drilled in the end of a bat and lead put in, make sure that it is securely fastened. Another popular item these days is the doughnut, a piece of circular metal tubing that is clamped on the barrel of the bat by passing it over the handle. The obvious advantage of using the doughnut is that the hitter gets a better feel for the swing by using his or her own bat.

Wind Sprints

These are very unpopular but, nevertheless, valuable exercises in which runners simply run as fast as they can from a standing start to a point less than a hundred yards away. It is best to simulate game conditions as well as possible by having the runner start the way he or she would if he or she had just hit the ball. The exercise can be made more realistic by placing a base at an appropriate distance. Additionally, having more than one player do a wind sprint at the same time can increase a player's speed since he or she will be competing with a teammate.

Infield

Every team should assemble its players early enough before a game to conduct a good round of infield. The idea is to simply put all the infielders at their proper position and then serve each a number of grounders. In turn, the fielders should make all the throws they will face in a game—to first base, second, third, and home—at one point in the exercise. The idea is to serve up every situation they may face in a game and then finish with "live grounders," with fielders not being told where these will be hit.

Outfield

The rules are the same as those for infield. It is a good idea to give the outfielders balls at varying heights so they can test possible conflicts with the sun, lights, or other background conditions. Also, be sure to give outfielders a good serving of grounders so they can test the surface of the ground. Don't forget: when a ground ball gets past an outfielder, it usually means a run. Hitting balls to outfielders can be enlivened by having the appropriate cutoff people getting into position to take the throws.

Burma Road

This is an old drill, designed to improve your running. The team's players all sprint to first base, then form a single line and jog around the bases until they all reach home plate. Next, the runners—one at a time—sprint from home plate to second base, where they gather to again jog homeward. Next, the runners sprint from home plate to third, where they jog home. Finally, they sprint all around the bases.

Pick-Up Drill

This is a good drill, both as a conditioner and for sharpening skills and concentration. It takes two players. One rolls two balls, one following the other, to the second player—first to one side, then the other. The idea is for the thrower to get the fielder moving back and forth as quickly as possible without making the throws uncatchable.

Fungo Drill

It is always a good idea to add a little zest to drills, and here is a good one to use for that purpose. In this particular drill a fungo hitter and at least six fielders are needed. The fielders line up on the left or right field foul lines. The first player starts running as fast as he or she can to the opposite foul line. When the fielder gets about halfway, the fungo hitter swats the ball in front of him or her toward the line at which he or she is headed. The idea is to see which of the fielders can be the most successful at making catches.

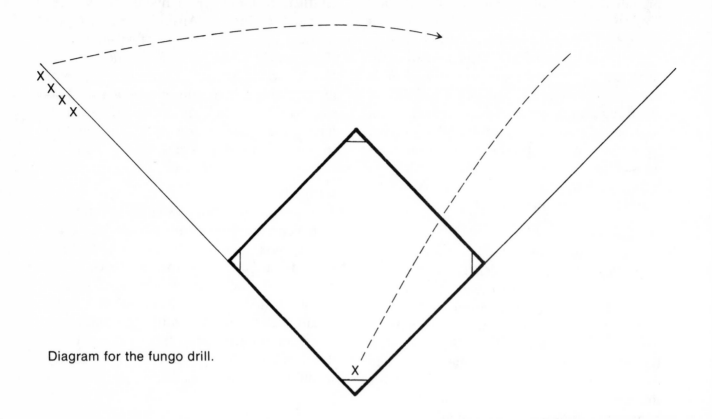

Diagram for the fungo drill.

13 Strategy

Many persons approach softball as strictly a bat-and-ball, field-and-throw sport. They think all there is to the game is for a player to try his or her best to get a hit when at the plate or to make the cleanest pickup and toss possible when on the field.

In reality, the good teams put considerably more into the game because there are plenty of opportunities to employ well-thought-out strategy. This is especially true on defense, where the proper deployment of the infielders and outfielders can go a long way toward enhancing the odds for victory.

There are some situations that generate basic, standard movements for the defense. For instance, with a runner on first and a batted ball to the third baseman, the second baseman (or short center fielder in some slow-pitch situations) automatically moves to second base to take the throw, tag the base, and make the relay toss to first base.

Or, say nobody is on base and the batter taps a grounder far to the right of the first baseman. When the first baseman makes the grab, it is automatic that the pitcher has moved to the bag to take a throw.

These types of movements are the best-known and most used, but there also occur—with a little imagination—many opportunities to use variations.

In most cases, the idea is to pit strength against strength. It is the goal of the defense to take away the offense's highest-percentage move by typically matching it with the best part of the defense. In the process, it is almost always advisable to deploy a team's strongest, most versatile fielders in the positions where they will see the most action.

For example, if the team at bat figures to hit a lot of balls up the middle, the club on the field would be best advised to deploy its best fielders at shortstop, second base, center field, and pitcher, as well as short center field in slow-pitch ball.

If the team at bat figures to have its many right-handed batters pull the ball a lot, then the defense will want to consider stationing its best fielders at third base, shortstop, and left field, as well as shading an extra outfielder into left.

In slow-pitch, the extra fielder easily could be moved to a spot behind the shortstop or just to the left side of second base since this person represents a manager's "wild card" who can be moved liberally around the field to plug the holes.

The following are some specific plays used by successful slow-pitch teams that, with a great deal of practice, can provide the winning edge.

BACKUP CATCHER

In slow-pitch softball, whether it is 12-inch or 16-inch, there almost always is one player on the team who is an exceptional hitter but of very dubious ability as a fielder. Invariably, the best place on the field for this player is catcher, since this is the spot where the fewest difficult plays occur during a contest.

However, since most of the plays that do occur at the plate—such as applying the tag to a runner trying to score—directly involve the scoring of a run, it is vital to be prepared to have a support plan for the catcher.

The best, most simple idea is for the pitcher to come to home plate to take the throws for the close plays with the catcher serving as his or her backup person. Another idea, when the pitcher is better employed at another task—such as backing up third on an extra-base hit—it may be advisable for the first baseman to come to the plate to receive the throw.

On occasion, it is not necessary to have two people at home plate for a defensive play. This occurs when there are large backstops close to the plate which serve as adequate backup support. In this case, it is advisable to avoid congestion and have the catcher vacate the area while the pitcher or first baseman covers the plate. The catcher, in turn, also can be used as a backup person at third base.

TENTH PLAYER

Slow-pitch softball gives managers a unique opportunity to stack a defense because of the use of a tenth fielder.

Typically, in 12-inch slow-pitch this extra person is used as a fourth outfielder with the outfield territory to be covered divided equally among the four players, each stationed equidistant from each other and at the same depth. In 16-inch, this player is customarily placed directly behind second base, occasionally moving slightly to the left or right in the case of a pull-hitter.

It is a wise manager who shifts this extra player around to shut down the changing strengths of the team at bat.

In 12-inch, it is not advisable to bring the extra outfielder all the way into the infield unless it is an absolute certainty that the batter is not capable of hitting the ball past infielders. But that rarely happens in 12-inch, and because of the hitter's ability to almost always knock the softball to the outfield, the tenth player should usually be played past the infield.

The astute manager uses the extra fielder at varying depths in 12-inch slow-pitch. Three deep outfielders should be able to cover the long, high flies which generally are turned into the majority of putouts during a game. Therefore, the best use of the tenth person is to cut off the dangerous line-drive hits just over the reach of the infielders.

For instance, in the case of a right-handed, line-drive batter, a good spot to place the extra fielder is in shallow left field

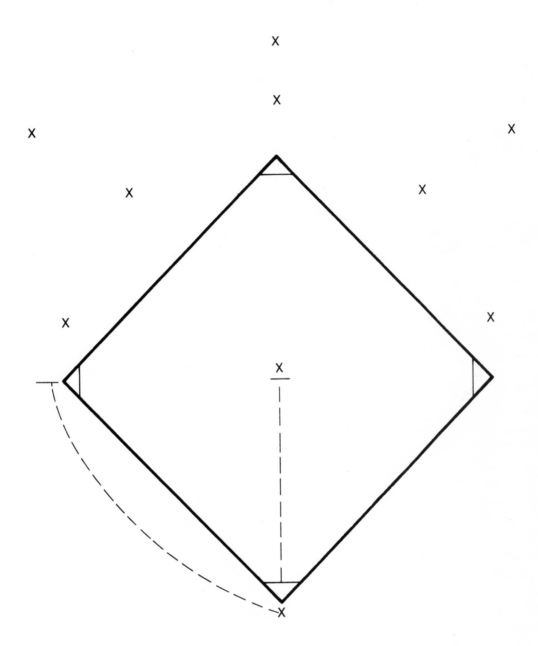

Diagram shows pitcher moving to home plate to cover for catcher, who moves to back up third base.

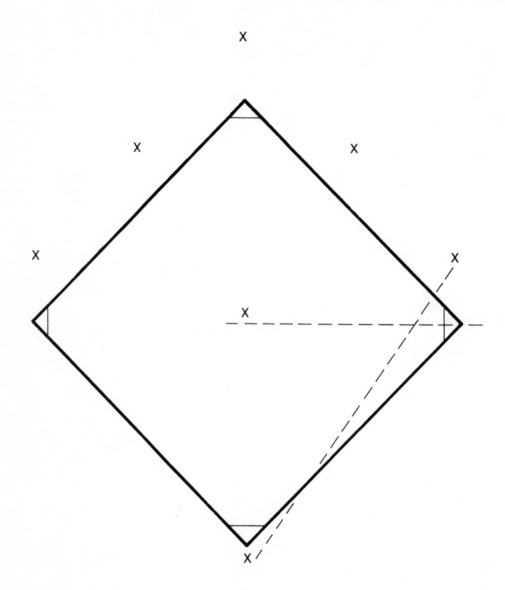

Here the pitcher moves to cover first base while the first baseman goes to the plate to serve as a back-up man or to cover for a play.

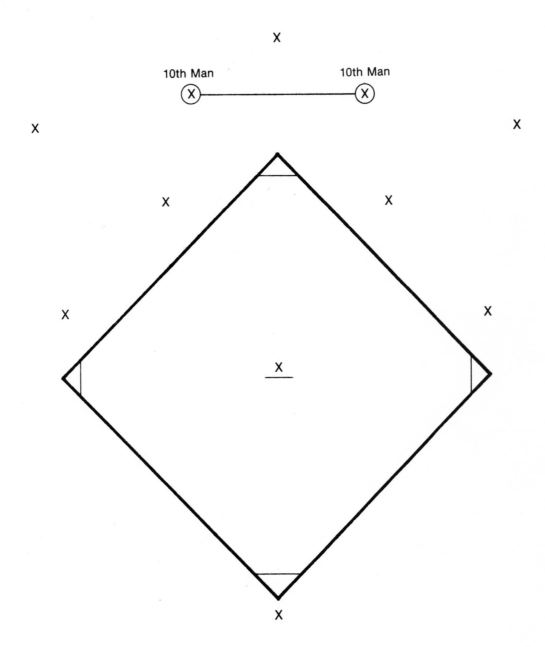

A good move in 12-inch slow-pitch can be to position the extra fielder shallower than the other outfielders as a plug for the power alleys.

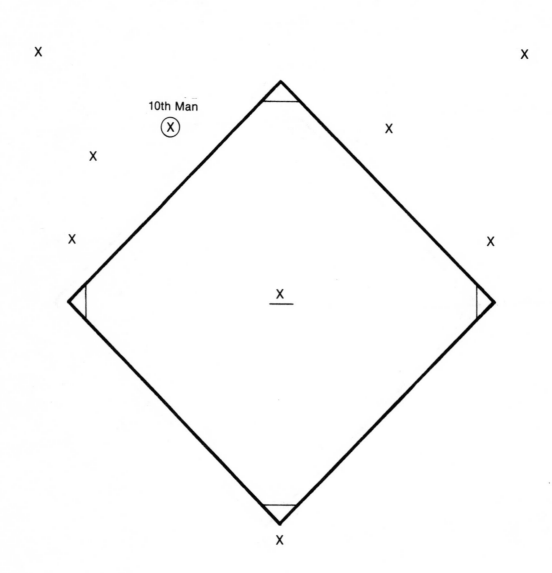

Sometimes in 16-inch slow-pitch the extra fielder is used as an auxiliary shortstop **against** a strong right-handed pull hitter.

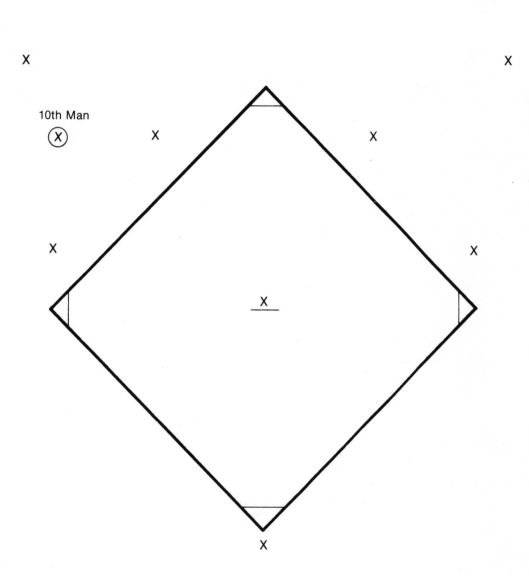

Here, also in 16-inch slow-pitch, the tenth fielder is being used to plug the area just over the infielders' heads on the left side.

while the deep left fielder shades closer to the foul line and the deep center fielder moves a few steps to his or her right. If the batter is a strong hitter up the middle, put the extra person in shallow center field and shaded either just to the right or left, depending on the latest tendencies of the person at the plate.

In 16-inch, it is more difficult to swat the really dangerous long flies that are so common to 12-inch and, therefore, the extra fielder almost always is used closer to the infield—usually just as an extra infielder.

The standard positioning for this person is directly behind second base, but it is smart sometimes to shift this person farther to the left or right in certain situations to completely shut down the side of an infield to the batter. Also, whereas in 12-inch it is progressive thinking to move the extra fielder closer to the infield, it sometimes is a very bold and effective move to shift the extra deeper into the outfield—such as in the shallow portions of the power alleys and sometimes even all the way over behind first or third base when trying to outmaneuver a batter who strictly pulls the ball when swinging.

PITCHER AS FIELDER

Increasingly, slow-pitch managers are recognizing the value of the pitcher as someone other than a person who just throws the ball to the plate.

It already has been discussed how this person can be used as a backup person at home plate or third, but he or she also

should be considered being deployed as an extra infielder. This is made especially feasible because of the slow lobs he or she uses for pitches and the time this allows for scrambling to a spot in the infield to be ready for grounders.

For instance, when an infield is shifted heavily toward the left side of the field, the pitcher, after releasing the ball, can take quick steps backward and toward right field to serve as a shallow second baseman for the regular second baseman who has shifted closer to the bag. The opposite would be true for a shift in the other direction, the pitcher becoming a shallow shortstop. (A warning: the pitcher should never try to make what would be a sensational stop of a ball when he or she knows there is another fielder behind in a position to make an easier play.)

In 12-inch slow-pitch, where the tenth player usually is stationed deeper than in 16-inch, the typical, sound strategy is to have the pitcher take steps directly backward toward second base to be in a better position to choke off grounders up the middle. However, as in 16-inch, the pitcher here also can backpedal diagonally to compensate for a second baseman or shortstop in a radical shift.

All of these movements require the pitcher to be especially agile and, for the team that plans to move the pitcher around a lot, it is a good idea to have a well-conditioned person playing the position. A fatigued pitcher can be costly late in the action when his or her control begins to waver and bases on balls are the result.

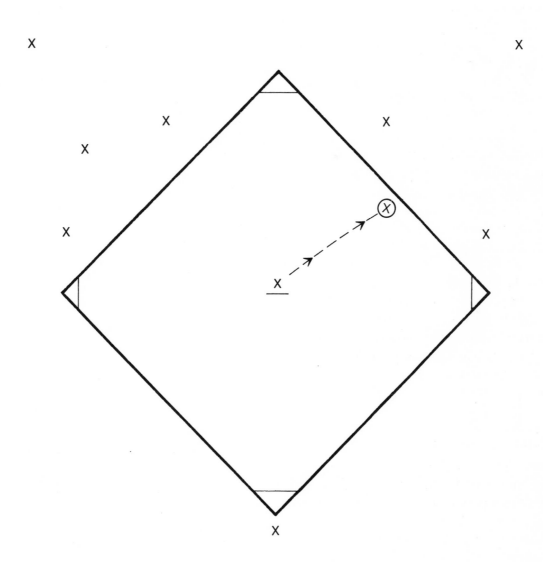

This diagram shows how the pitcher moves, in this case toward second base, to serve as an extra infielder.

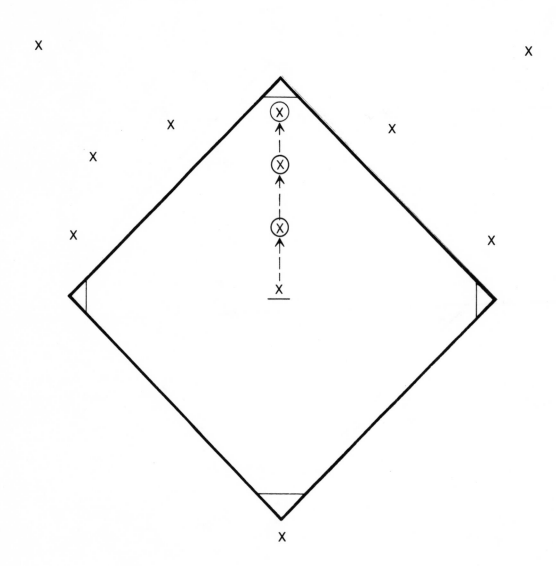

Here is the most common move of all for a pitcher, whether it is in 12-inch or 16-inch slow-pitch.

The most common deployment of fielders in 12-inch slow-pitch. However, it should not necessarily be considered a fixture.

Glossary

Appeal Play—A play when an umpire cannot make a decision until requested by a player or coach. The request must be made before the next pitch. The four typical appeals are: (1) batting out of order; (2) leaving a base before a fly ball is touched; (3) not touching a base, or touching out of order; (4) overrunning first base and then being tagged on the attempt to go to second.

Assist—A play in which a fielder helps action that puts a runner out.

At Bat—A completed turn at the plate by a batter.

Base on Balls—When a batter is awarded first base following four pitches that are judged by the umpire as balls.

Base Path—A imaginary line 3 feet on either side of a direct line between bases.

Base Runner—A player on a team at bat who has reached at least first base.

Bat—The instrument used by a batter to strike the ball; it can be either wood or metal.

Batter—The player on an offensive team who faces the pitcher.

Batter's Box—The area adjacent to home plate to which the batter is restricted while facing the pitcher.

Battery—The combination of a team's pitcher and catcher.

Batting Average—The number of hits divided by the number of times at bat; the result, usually expressed in three decimals, shows a player's proficiency as a hitter.

Batting Order—The official listing of a team's players in the sequence they will appear at the plate.

Box Score—A statistical account in condensed form of a completed game.

Breaking Pitch—A ball, delivered by the pitcher, that curves.

Bunt—A legally struck ball in which the hitter does not take a full swing and tries to keep the ball within the infield.

Catcher—The defensive player behind home plate whose main responsibility is to receive balls thrown by the pitcher.

Chance—A term for attempting a play.

Change-Up—The varying of the speed of the ball by a pitcher, geared at disrupting the batter's timing.

Chopper—A high-bouncing batted ball.

Chucker—The pitcher.

Cleanup Hitter—The batter who is number four in the lineup; typically, a person who hits the ball long distances.

Closed Stance—When the hitter places the front foot closer to the plate than the back foot as he or she waits for a delivery.

Coach—Members of the team who stand near first and third base to give baserunning instruction; also can be a person who gives instruction to a team on other phases of the sport.

Count—The number of balls and strikes on a batter.

Curve—A pitched ball that does not move in a straight line.

Cutoff Man—A player who intercepts a ball thrown to a teammate.

Dead Ball—When a ball legally is no longer in play.

Defensive Team—The team on the field.

Delivery—A pitch.

Diamond—Area formed by the four bases.

Double—A base hit that enables the batter to reach second base despite perfect fielding by the defense.

Double Play—When the defense retires two offensive players in continuous action.

Double Steal—When two runners steal bases on the same play.

E.R.A.—The average number of earned runs which a pitcher allows during a full game.

Error—A mistake by a defensive player that allows a batter to remain at bat longer than he or she should, a base runner to remain on base longer than he or she should, or that allows a runner to reach base or take an extra base. (A base on balls, wild pitch, or passed ball do not count.)

Extra-Base Hit—Any hit more than a single.

Fair Ball—Any legally batted ball which is not foul. To be judged fair, a ball must stop or be touched in fair territory between home plate and first base or home plate and third base; or a ball which is inside either foul line when bouncing past first or third; or a ball which first hits on or inside either foul line on a fly past first or third base.

Fielder—Any player of the team in the field.

Fielder's Choice—A play in which a player in the field opts to throw to a base other than first for an out.

First Baseman—The defensive player who covers the territory around first base.

Fly Ball—A ball that is hit into the air, usually to the outfield.

Force Out—To retire a runner by touching the next base he or she is forced to advance to.

Foul Ball—A batted ball that is judged not fair.

Full Count—When there are three balls and two strikes on the hitter.

Glove—Equipment used by fielders as an aid in catching the ball.

Grand Slam—A home run with a runner on each base.

Grounder—A batted ball that hits the ground as it leaves the bat.

Hit—Reaching a base safely on a batted ball that is not misplayed by the defense.

Home Run—A base hit on which the batter touches all bases without the ball being misplayed.

Home Team—Defined as the host team, which bats in the bottom half of an inning.

Hook Slide—A baserunning maneuver in which the runner, trying to reach a base on a close play, slides feet first into the base and twists the body away from the defensive player, touching the base with the rear foot.

Infield—Fair territory bounded by the base paths.

Infielder—A defensive player who plays in the infield.

Infield Fly—A fair ball that does not hit the ground and can be caught by an infielder.

Infield Hit—A base hit that does not go past an infielder.

Inning—A division of a game, divided into halves that allow each team to bat and field once apiece; similar to the frame in bowling.

Interference—When a player hinders or prevents an opponent from making a play.

Lead Off—The batter who starts his team's turn at the plate; or, to move off a base before the ball is pitched.

Line Drive—A hard-hit ball that stays on a relatively straight line instead of going skyward before hitting the ground.

Mask—Safety equipment, worn by the catcher, that straps on his or her head and covers the face.

Mitt—Generally meaning the glove worn by a catcher or first baseman in which the thumb portion is separate from the rest of the glove.

Obstruction—When a fielder not holding or fielding the ball hinders the progress of a base runner.

Offensive Team—The team at bat.

On-Deck Batter—The batter who follows the teammate who is at the plate.

On-Deck Circle—The area in foul territory designated as the place for the on-deck batter to warm up.

Out—The retirement of a batter or base runner. Each team is allowed three outs during its time at bat.

Outfield—Fair territory beyond the infield.

Outfielder—A player positioned in the outfield.

Passed Ball—A legally pitched ball that the catcher fails to control despite its not having been hit.

Perfect Game—A contest in which the pitcher allows no opposing player to reach base in a complete game.

Pickoff—The trapping of a runner off base by a sudden throw.

Pinch Hitter—A batter substituted for another batter already in the lineup.

Pitcher—The defensive player who starts each play by throwing the ball to home plate.

Pitching Rubber—The rubber or wood rectangle on which the pitcher starts each delivery.

Pop-Up—A fly ball, either foul or fair, which can be easily caught.

Pull Hitter—A batter who consistently hits the ball to the nearest side of the field.

Quick Pitch—A throw to the plate by the pitcher that arrives quicker than normally expected by the batter.

RBI—A run batted in.

Relay—The return of the ball from the outfield by an intermediate defensive player.

Relay Man—A fielder who takes a throw from a teammate and throws it to another fielder.

Riseball—A pitched ball that deviates from a straight line by moving upward.

Run—A unit of scoring.

Rundown—A defensive maneuver in which two or more defensive players attempt to tag a base runner trapped between bases.

Sacrifice—The advancement of a base runner by the batter deliberately hitting the ball in such a manner that the defensive team can make a play only on the batter.

Second Baseman—The defensive player stationed in the infield on the right side of second base.

Shortstop—The defensive player stationed in the infield on the left side of second base.

Shutout—When a pitcher prevents the opposition from scoring any runs during a contest.

Single—A base hit on which the batter reaches first base.

Slide—The act of a base runner sliding along the ground toward a base to prevent being put out.

Slingshot—A style of delivery used by pitchers in fast-pitch in which the throwing arm does not make a full circle.

Spikes—Rubber, plastic, or metal cleats attached to a player's shoes to provide better traction.

Squeeze Play—An offensive move in which a runner on third base runs for home plate as the hitter attempts to bunt.

Steal—The advancement to the next base solely by baserunning, that is, without a hit necessarily being made.

Strike—A ball thrown by the pitcher which enters the strike zone.

Strike Zone—In slow-pitch, generally defined as that space over any portion of home plate between the batter's highest shoulder and knees, when assuming a natural stance; in fast-pitch, that space over any portion of home plate between the batter's armpits and top of the knees, when assuming a natural stance.

Tag—The touching of a runner with the ball or with a glove that holds the ball, for the purpose of putting the runner out.

Third Baseman—The defensive player who guards the area around third base.

Triple—A base hit in which the batter reaches third base.

Triple Play—When three offensive players are put out in continuous action.

Walk—A base on balls.

Warm-Up—The time used in exercise or practice by players in preparation for a game.

Wild Pitch—A ball legally delivered to the plate by the pitcher but so inaccurate that it cannot be controlled by the catcher.

Windmill—A style of delivery by a pitcher in fast-pitch in which the throwing arm makes a complete circle.

Windup—The pitcher's movements in preparation for throwing the ball to a batter.

Index